# Eating Cuban

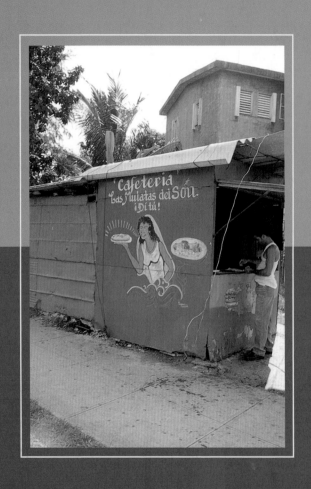

# Eating Cuban

**BEVERLY COX** AND **MARTIN JACOBS**

Introduction by Ana Menéndez

Stewart, Tabori & Chang   New York

*To Craig Jacobs, whose love of all things Cuban inspired us.*

回 回 回

Editor: Marisa Bulzone
Designer: Laura Lindgren
Production Manager: Jane Searle

Library of Congress Cataloging-in-Publication Data
Cox, Beverly
   Eating Cuban : 120 authentic recipes from the
streets of Havana to American shores / Beverly Cox
and Martin Jacobs ; Introduction by Ana Menéndez.
      p.   cm.
   Includes bibliographical references and index.
   ISBN 1-58479-541-7
   1. Cookery, Cuban.  I. Jacobs, Martin. II. Title.
TX716.C8C69 2006
641.597291—dc22                              2006008795

Published in 2006 by Stewart, Tabori & Chang
An imprint of Harry N. Abrams, Inc.

The text of this book was composed in Pacella, Interstate, and Berber.

Printed in Thailand
10 9 8 7 6 5 4 3 2 1

**HNA** ▪▪▪▪▪
**harry n. abrams, inc.**
a subsidiary of La Martinière Groupe

115 West 18th Street
New York, NY 10011
www.hnabooks.com

# Contents

  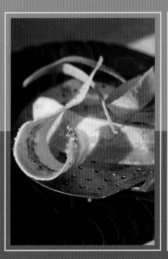  

# Preface

My grandmothers, May Cox and Elizabeth Walker, loved to travel. They were both widows and, though quite different in personality, compatible travel companions. Every year after the Christmas holidays, they embarked on a train journey around the United States that impressed me, as a small child, because the excursion tickets were so long that they stretched across the room. A high point of the trip was a cruise from Miami to Havana, where they would spend a few days touring the island. Cuba, as they described it to the family in vivid detail, was a tropical paradise with great food and hospitable people who showed special kindness to senior citizens and children. I remember plotting to convince my parents that visiting Cuba with the Grandmas would be much more educational than school, but my dream trip never materialized.

In the 1950s, when Havana was a popular tourist destination, no one would have believed that an island ninety miles off the coast of Florida would soon become less accessible to Americans than Tibet or Timbuktu. And yet, part of Cuba's special appeal today is just that:, it has been off limits for so long. Naturally then, I was intrigued when Marty Jacobs told me that his son Craig, who is a chef, had been traveling to Havana on business. When he brought up the possibility that we could legally accompany Craig as food consultants and explore the cooking of modern Cuba, I started mentally packing my suitcase.

Cuba has a rich culinary history that reflects the influences of Native American, Spanish, African, Chinese, and French immigrations. From what we have found on our trips to Havana, the food at most tourist hotels is not great, but good Cuban cooking can still be found at *paladares* (private restaurants), some of which are very elegant and others just simple take-out windows in people's homes. People in the countryside also eat well because they grow a lot of their own food. Since meat, particularly beef, is still hard to come by in the cities, there are also some interesting vegetarian restaurants where the chefs cook with local produce.

Over the past fifty years, wherever Cubans have settled in the United States, their food has had an impact. This is especially true in Florida cities like Tampa and Miami, where it is very popular. Among the dishes that have become American favorites are Cuban black bean soup, *tostones* (double deep-fried green plaintain chips), *empanadas* (pastry turnovers filled with spicy beef filling), *sandwich Cubano* (a toasted submarine sandwich), *ropa vieja* (shredded beef in tomato sauce), *Moros y Cristianos* (black beans and rice), and *flan* (Cuban caramel custard).

On our travels to Cuba we have been very fortunate to meet many kind and hospitable people. Some great Cuban cooks, both professional and amateur, have generously shared their knowledge and recipes with us. In spite of frequent difficulties in obtaining ingredients, creative cooks seem able to prevail. And we hope that the photographs will help readers appreciate the flavor and beauty of the island.

Marty and I would like to thank our friends in Cuba: Rafael and his wonderful family, Justo and Rosario. David, Lucy, Isabel and Frank, Eduardo, Alicia and Ellie, Alejandro and Amarilis, Hubert and Manolo, Raquel, Madelaine, Maria Elena, Carmen and Enrique, Beatriz and Jaime, Susana and the two Jorges, Marta, Juan Carlos and Lidia Olga.

And we have met many great Cuban-American cooks, particularly in Miami, Tampa and Gulfport, Florida, and Hoboken, New Jersey, who have shared their recipes and knowledge of the exciting Cuban food scene in the United States. Many thanks to Juanita Plana, Lucila Venet Jimenez, Virginia Flores-Godoy and Gustavo Godoy, Maricel Presilla, Josefa Gonzales-Hastings, Douglas Rodriguez, Jorge and Tamara Salt, Sixto Delgado, Dan Cuñado, Luis and Juanita Tejada, and "Majito" Aguila.

Writing and publishing a cookbook requires the efforts of many people. This project would not have been possible without the help of Craig and Michelle Jacobs.

We would like to thank our spouses, Linda Johnson, who, as always, did a wonderful job of styling the photographs, and Gordon Black, who typed and organized the manuscript. My friend, and the world's best test cook, Judy Day was a joy to work with. This project also brought to my attention another great Cuban-American cook, Barbara Trujillo, who tested the recipes in the drinks chapter and acted as an on-site Cuban consultant for the book. My mother, Betty Cox, and the Day and Trujillo families were excellent tasters, and we appreciated their input.

Ana Menéndez, eloquent as always, wrote a wonderful introduction. Our agent Judith Weber, and publisher Leslie Stoker and editor Marisa Bulzone at Stewart, Tabori and Chang, have encouraged and supported us from the beginning and shared our excitement about the rare opportunity we had to visit Cuba. Many thanks also to copy editor Liana Krissoff, who converted recipes and text into a polished manuscript and to designer Laura Lindgren, who wove all of the visual and editorial elements into a finished book that pleased us all.

Our travels—and the creation of this book—have been a great culinary adventure and we are eager to share it with you.

*Buen Provecho!*
Beverly Cox and Martin Jacobs

# Introduction

by Ana Menéndez

My favorite Cuban delicacy isn't really the stuff of fine cookbooks. It was born not in a test kitchen but in that creative cauldron called the screw-up. "Raspita" is the crunchy toasted rice at the bottom of a pot that's been left too long on the heat. After you scrape it up, raspita's nutty crackle becomes the perfect foil to a bowl of soft steaming rice. Delicious and forgiving, raspita is a fine reminder that there is joy even in error and that sometimes an excess of competence can yield its own kind of hunger.

Every rice-eating culture has its version of raspita. But for me there could be no finer standard-bearer for Cuban food, a "cuisine" that is, at its best, unpretentious, unexpected, and infinitely gracious in its willingness to adapt, especially when it comes to bad luck.

And Cuba has had more than its fair helping of bad luck: Wars, famines, coups, and revolutions. Fat cow years followed by lean cow years, followed by more hunger, followed by gilded plenty and back again.

Food, the getting it, the cooking it, the enjoying it, became such a national obsession that the Cubans learned to describe a wide range of feeling and circumstance using the language of the dinner table: An annoying person made your life a yogurt. Pleasant, entertaining lies were guavas. And if you were inclined to be too accommodating, a good friend might remind you that she who makes herself honey-sweet will be eaten by the ants.

After the collapse of the Soviet Union, Cuba descended into a "special period" that tested even the limits of Cuban inventiveness.

Cats were said to have disappeared from the cities. In the countryside, cows needed to be watched carefully, lest a butcher thief came in the night and hacked a leg off a live animal. And urban lore created a new Cuban dish: breaded kitchen rag. I never saw it and can't vouch for its existence. But supposedly, it tasted a lot like steak, hunger seasoning the palate as well as the imagination.

In exile, with its excess of *pastelitos*, food served primarily as fuel for nostalgia. Many in my generation grew up eating black beans, mangoes, and beef that wasn't even the sandal of what our parents had enjoyed in Cuba.

"In Cuba the soil was so rich," my mother used to tell me, "that if you spit a seed out a car window, when you returned there'd be a tree growing in its place."

Somehow we made do with our inferior American versions and managed to grow fat on memories. I spent summers at my godparents' chewing sugarcane. Christmas Eve was celebrated with roast pork. Eating was at the center of family life and no occasion, no matter how small, was ever celebrated without food, even if it was just a plate of little deviled-ham sandwiches. In high school, the boys used to smack their lips and say: "If you cook the way you walk, I'll eat even the raspita."

❖ ❖ ❖

As I grew older, my annoyance with the Cuban nostalgia machine extended itself to the food. I declared myself disgusted with the narrow Cuban tastes of my upbringing, the unwillingness to experiment, the insistence on rehashing the same old dishes and the same old stories. I became, briefly, a food deviant: dabbling in foams and tiny shot-glasses of "paella soup." But everyone comes home eventually. And I could never, no matter how much I tried, entirely escape my mother's kitchen. Because that's where I learned to be a writer.

This shouldn't seem strange. Cuban food is not fancy. It consists of a limited number of plot devices, endlessly retold. Black beans and white rice, yuca, fresh okra and squash, some good helpings of meat (always overcooked), some hearty stews. Each dish comes with its own backstory: the white rice from the Chinese, the yuca from the native islanders, vegetables from the African slaves, stews from the Spanish.

In this country many seem to regard "Cuban food" as something that came out of the island wholly formed. But Cubans know it is a creative mix that reflects both the country's own cultural provenance as well as its sordid and glorious history: of slavery and indentured servitude as well as of hope and sanctuary.

Like all peasant cuisines, traditional Cuban food walks wide of innovation and hews close to the known, the principle of a good meal lying snugly between sustenance and honest pleasure. Simplicity as the height of good taste: A fine lesson for a budding writer to sop up with her white bean stew.

In my mother's kitchen I learned the importance of letting things develop over time. Of adapting to the ingredients at hand. Of making mistakes delicious. Writing is not a pleasure in and of itself—any more than working all day over a hot stove is. The pleasure comes in the eating. And the good cook will put up with burnt fingers and surface wounds for the pleasure of something fresh and beautifully made.

The book you hold in your hands is a sweet and honest love letter to Cuban food. For those coming to the Cuban table for the first time, the recipes offer a straight and simple roadmap to the cuisine. For those who grew up with picadillo and arroz con pollo, the recipes will send you tumbling back to recollection.

The *Palitos de Yuca Frita* on page 67 brought back memories of Christmas day, when all the leftover yuca from the *Noche Buena* meal would be fried and kept warm in the oven for passing nibblers. The lovely recipes with harina reminded me of cool afternoons in Tampa, pouring sugar and milk into steaming bowls of the stuff. I made some just the other day to serve with braised chicken. I stirred mascarpone cheese into it and called it polenta, with just a tad of shame.

Exile did not work out exactly as our parents had planned. For their American children, Cuba is little more than a fairy-tale land of perfect fruit and blue hills. Every year the island and whatever promise it once held for us slips farther out of reach. What we have left is the food. And most days, that seems gift enough.

# ONE | Las Raices ▣ The Roots

# Las Raices | The Roots

"Cuba is an *ajiaco*" is an old Cuban saying that refers both to Cuba's national dish, a stew made with many different vegetables and meats, and to the diverse cultures that came together to forge the Cuban character.

The name *Cuba* derives from the Ciboney word *itiba cahubaba*, which means "Mother Earth." The Ciboney and the Guanahatabey are the first known human inhabitants of Cuba. The Ciboney were fishermen and seafarers. Shell mounds, remnants of their civilizations, are still found throughout the islands of the Caribbean. They are thought to have originated on the North American mainland. The Guanahatabey were hunter-gatherers. Some anthropologists believe that they migrated to Cuba from the Yucatán Peninsula. What is known for sure is that Ciboney and Guanahatabey settlements in Cuba date back several thousand years.

About five hundred years before the arrival of the Spanish in 1492, the Taino, another Native American group, migrated north to Cuba from the Orinoco Basin of South America. The Taino were farmers and hunters. Using an old Amazonian farming method, they grew yuca (cassava), *maíz* (corn), beans, squash, sweet potatoes, *ajies* (peppers), annatto seed, cotton, and tobacco in *conucos*, parcels of land with mounds of earth packed with leaves to prevent soil erosion. Combining the vegetables and *ajies* they harvested with whatever fish or game was at hand, they made a stew called *ajiaco*.

Until recently, most Cubans would tell you that all of the Indians in Cuba were killed in the sixteenth century by the Spanish invaders and by the introduction of diseases like smallpox, to which they had no immunity. It's true that the native peoples of Cuba suffered greatly under the Spanish occupation. Those who survived did so by keeping a low profile. They adopted Spanish customs and often intermarried with the Spanish and later with Cimarrones, runaway African slaves. Their customs and beliefs were not forgotten, however: Like the Africans, the Amerindians adopted Spanish Catholicism, but managed to meld their own beliefs with Catholic ritual. It is no coincidence that the Catholic celebration of Cuba's patron saint, Nuestra Señora de la Caridad del Cobre, that is held in September with processions, masses, and feasts, coincides with the Ciboney celebration of *atabeyra,* the Ciboney Mother of the Ocean and the Earth.

Spain was a powerful influence in the development of Cuban cooking. Starting in the sixteenth century, Peninsulares (immigrants from Spain) came to Cuba, lured by the island's beauty and economic possibilities. They imported domestic animals and poultry and planted Old World fruit trees and crops. They brought with them their favorite ingredients, like olive oil, capers, cumin, oregano, bay leaves, and saffron, and recipes for traditional Spanish dishes like flan, *tortilla española*, *caldo gallego*, paella, and *arroz con pollo*.

In 1790, a slave uprising in Haiti drove thousands of French planters and their households to Cuba. They settled on the eastern side of the island and established coffee plantations. The French influence in Cuban cooking is evident in the *pastelitos* and other baked goods that are specialties in the eastern provinces.

There had been African slaves in Cuba since the sixteenth century, but the slave trade reached its height in the eighteenth and nineteenth centuries. Sugar and tobacco were Cuba's main exports, and the Native American workforce was so diminished by that time that the Spanish and French planters began to import large numbers of African slaves to work on the sugar, coffee, and cacao plantations.

The slaves came from several different African culture groups. The majority were Bantu, from south of the Equator, and Yoruba, from southwestern Nigeria. Africans brought with them foods like *ñame* (African yam), okra, and plantains and also *malanga isleña* (white- and yellow-fleshed taro root) and peanuts, two plants that had originated in South America but came to Cuba via Nigeria. These Africans adopted the foods they found in Cuba and added their own touches. They were the cooks on most plantations and were largely responsible for the development of Cuban creole cooking. Words like *congrí* (red or black beans and rice), *fufú* (mashed plantains), and *calalú* (meat soup with pot herbs) are all African in origin.

By the mid-nineteenth century, the Spanish were coming under international pressure to discontinue the importation of slaves. Planters in Cuba, searching for an alternate labor force, looked to China. In 1847 the first of many shiploads of coolies (indentured servants) from China arrived in Havana from Guangdong Province. After fulfilling their eight-year work contracts, most of these men stayed on and, often, married African slaves. Between 1860 and 1875, another, more prosperous group of Chinese immigrants arrived, from California. Many Chinese opened restaurants and ice cream stands, and Chinese seasonings like ginger and star anise, and dishes like fried rice, took on new Cuban identities.

Cuba's history is exotic, and so is its food. The blending of traditional Spanish recipes and cooking techniques with Amerindian, African, and Asian ingredients and influences has resulted in a creole cuisine that is distinctly Cuban and very much an *ajiaco*.

# Ajiaco
## Traditional Meat and Vegetable Stew

**A**jiaco is a dish with deep roots in Cuban history. Its origins can be traced back to the Ciboney and Taino people who inhabited the island before the arrival of the Spanish in the late fifteenth century. These Native Americans were fishermen, farmers, and hunters. Among the crops that they grew in mounded beds called *conucos* were yuca (cassava), *maíz* (corn), *boniato* (white sweet potato), calabaza (West Indian pumpkin), and *ajíes* (hot chiles).

The first *ajiacos* were stews that combined these vegetables with whatever fish or small game—like *jutía* (a kind of possum)—was available. Over the centuries, the dish evolved as new ingredients were added by different ethnic groups. From the Spanish came pork, beef, olive oil, garlic, cumin, and citrus fruits like bitter Seville oranges and limes. Africans introduced *malanga* (white- and yellow-fleshed taro root), *ñame* (African yam), and plantains.

*Ajiaco* is the kind of dish that is kept continuously simmering on the back of the stove with ingredients added from time to time to replenish the pot. It is considered Cuba's national dish.

Serve the *Ajiaco* with *Pan de Cazabé* (Modern Cassava [Yuca] Bread; page 37).

Soak the *tasajo* for several hours or overnight in several changes of cold water.

Drain the *tasajo* and place it in a large soup pot with the broth or water and bay leaves. Cover and bring to a boil over medium-high heat. Add the skirt steak, pork, and short ribs; reduce the heat to low. Cover and simmer for 1 hour, or until the meats are tender, stirring occasionally and skimming off any foam that rises to the surface. Remove the cooked meats from the broth, reserving the broth. Skim off and discard as much fat as possible from the top of the broth. (If you have time, refrigerate the broth until the fat solidifies, then remove it.) When cool enough to handle, remove the rib meat from the bones and trim off any gristle and fat; cut the *tasajo*, skirt steak, and pork into bite-size chunks. Return the meat to the broth.

Meanwhile, make the sofrito: In a large skillet over medium heat, heat the oil. Add the onion and bell peppers and cook over medium-low heat, stirring often, until the onion is translucent, 5 to 7 minutes. Stir in the garlic, tomatoes, and cumin and continue to simmer for an additional 10 minutes. Add the sofrito to the soup pot.

*(continued)*

**FOR THE BROTH**

½ pound *tasajo* (salt dried beef)

4 quarts *Caldo de Res* (Beef Broth; page 46) or water

3 bay leaves

1 pound beef skirt steak or flank steak

1 pound pork shoulder

1 pound beef short ribs

**FOR THE SOFRITO**

¼ cup olive oil

2 cups (1 large) chopped onion

2 green bell peppers, seeded and chopped

1½ tablespoons (5 to 6 cloves) minced garlic

1 (15-ounce) can crushed tomatoes

2 teaspoons ground cumin, or to taste

## FOR THE STEW

½ pound (1 medium) white *malanga* (white-fleshed taro root)

¼ pound (1 small) yellow *malanga* (yellow-fleshed taro root)

1 pound (2 medium) *boniatos* (white sweet potatoes)

½ pound (½ small) *ñame* (African yam)

½ pound (1 small) yuca

1 green plantain (skin should be green to yellow)

1½ cups peeled, cubed calabaza or butternut squash

3 to 4 ears fresh corn, husked and cut into 1-inch rounds

1 ripe plantain (skin should be black)

2 tablespoons fresh lime juice

Salt to taste

Fresh lime wedges

*Salsa Picante de Don Justo* (Don Justo's Hot Sauce; page 51) or other hot pepper sauce to taste

While the meats are cooking, peel the *malanga*, *boniatos*, and *ñame* using a vegetable peeler. Cut the yuca in half lengthwise and remove the fibrous core that runs down the center of the tuber. Peel with a vegetable peeler, making sure to remove both the waxed outer peel and the rosy underpeel. This may also be done with a paring knife: Insert the tip of the knife under the peel and underpeel to loosen them, then use your hands to peel them off. Cut up the tubers and place them in a bowl of cold water so they won't discolor.

Add the tubers to the soup pot and simmer, covered, for 30 minutes.

With a sharp knife, make one lengthwise slash in the skin of the green plantain. Cut the plantain in 1-inch pieces, peel the skin from the pieces, and discard. Toss the plantain with the lime juice, then drain the plantain, reserving the lime juice.

Add the green plantain and calabaza to the stew. Continue to simmer, uncovered, for 15 minutes.

Add the corn and simmer for an additional 10 to 15 minutes, or until all of the ingredients are tender when pierced with the tip of a knife.

Meanwhile, slice off and discard about 1 inch at each end of the ripe plantain. With a sharp knife, cut a lengthwise slit through the skin, but do not remove the peel. Cut the plantain into ½-inch-thick slices and cook in simmering water to cover until tender, about 10 minutes. Drain the plantain and run under cold water until cool enough to handle. Peel the slices and add them to the stew.

Stir in the lime juice and season the stew with salt. Spoon the *Ajiaco* into soup plates and serve with lime wedges and *Salsa Picante de Don Justo* on the side.

SERVES 12.

# Caldo Gallego
## Galician White Bean Soup

1 cup dried white beans

7 ounces sliced Spanish chorizo

2 cups (1 large) chopped white onion

1¼ cups (1 large) chopped green bell
   pepper

3 or 4 large cloves garlic, peeled and
   minced or pressed

1 smoked ham hock

1 quart chicken or beef broth

1 bunch (about ½ pound) collard greens

3 red potatoes, peeled and cubed

Salt to taste

Many of the Spanish settlers who immigrated to Cuba between the sixteenth and nineteenth centuries were from the province of Galicia. *Caldo gallego* is a hearty peasant dish that remains popular in Cuba today.

If you have a pressure cooker, you may use it instead of the Dutch oven to speed up the cooking; see the instructions in the recipe for *Frijoles Negros* (Classic Cuban-Style Black Beans; page 47).

Rinse the beans under cold running water and place them in a saucepan with enough water to cover by 2 inches. Bring to a boil over high heat. Boil the beans for about 5 minutes. Remove from the heat and let the beans soak in the water overnight.

In a large Dutch oven over medium-low heat, cook the chorizo, stirring often, until it begins to render its fat. Remove the chorizo with a slotted spoon and set aside. Add the onion and bell pepper to the drippings and cook, stirring, until the onion is translucent and beginning to brown, about 10 minutes. Drain the beans and add them to the pot. Add the garlic, ham hock, broth, and 2 to 3 quarts water. Cover the pot and bring to a boil over medium-high heat. Reduce the heat to low and cook, covered, stirring occasionally, until the beans are tender, 1½ to 3 hours, depending upon the altitude at which you are cooking.

Meanwhile, rinse the collard greens thoroughly with cold water and drain. Remove and discard the tough stems, and tear the leaves into small pieces; set aside. When the beans are tender, add the chorizo, collard greens, and potatoes. Bring to a boil over medium-high heat. Reduce the heat to low and cook, covered, stirring occasionally, until the potatoes are tender. If necessary, add a little additional broth or water to the pot. If it seems like there is too much liquid, cook uncovered until it is reduced to your liking.

SERVES 6 AS A MAIN COURSE.

# Ensalada de Yuca Ciboney
## Ciboney-Style Yuca Salad

It was the Ciboney and Taino who first cultivated yuca in Cuba. It was their main vegetable staple before the Spanish invasion, and yuca was later adopted by Spanish and African cooks to became an important element in Cuban creole cooking.

The Ciboney and Taino also added European and African foods to their diet. In this typical Ciboney salad recipe, shared with us by Tamara and Jorge Luis Salt of the Ciboney Tribe of Florida, yuca, *ajies dulces* (mild peppers), and cilantro are dressed with Spanish olive oil, lime juice, and garlic and sprinkled with salt. (The Ciboney and Taino acquired salt through trade with their kinsmen in the Bahamas.)

Cut the yuca in half lengthwise and remove the fibrous core that runs down the center of the tuber. Peel with a vegetable peeler, making sure to remove both the waxed outer peel and the rosy underpeel. This may also be done with a paring knife: Insert the tip of the knife under the peel and underpeel to loosen them, then use your hands to peel them off. Place the peeled yuca in a large pot of boiling water and boil gently until the yuca starts to open up, about 20 minutes. Add 1 cup cold water and about 1 teaspoon salt. Continue to cook until the yuca is tender when pierced with a knife, about 10 minutes. Drain and rinse the yuca under cold running water, then drain and cut it into bite-size pieces. Place the yuca in a bowl with the pimientos and cilantro. Put the lime juice in a small bowl and gradually whisk in the oil. Pour the dressing over the yuca mixture and toss gently. Serve the salad on a bed of lettuce, if desired.

SERVES 4 TO 6.

1 pound fresh or frozen yuca
Salt to taste
1 (4-ounce) jar sliced pimientos, or
   1 roasted red bell pepper, thinly sliced
1 to 2 tablespoons chopped fresh
   cilantro or *culantro*
2 to 3 teaspoons fresh lime juice
   (optional)
3 to 4 tablespoons extra-virgin olive oil
1 head green leaf lettuce (optional)

# Arroz Frito
## Fried Rice

2 cups uncooked long-grain white rice,
  or 4 cups leftover cooked white rice

4 eggs

3 to 4 tablespoons peanut oil

¼ pound roast pork, cut into ¼-inch-
  thick slices

¼ pound ham, cut into ¼-inch-thick
  slices

¼ pound small fresh shrimp, cooked in
  boiling water

2 cloves garlic, peeled and lightly
  crushed

2 teaspoons minced fresh ginger

½ teaspoon Asian chile-garlic sauce
  (optional)

3 to 5 tablespoons soy sauce

2 green onions (green and white parts
  only), thinly sliced

1 tablespoon chopped fresh cilantro

The first Chinese immigrants arrived in Cuba as coolies (indentured servants), imported by Spanish settlers in the mid-1800s to work in the sugarcane fields. Most were men from the Chinese province of Guangdong. After their eight-year contracts were fulfilled, most stayed on, and settled in what was to become El Bario Chino de la Habana (Havana's Chinatown). As in the United States, many Chinese immigrants opened restaurants and made a definite impact on Cuban cooking. Today, fried rice is a dish that is routinely prepared by Cubans from all ethnic backgrounds.

Cook the rice a day in advance, or use leftover cooked rice.

Place the rice in a saucepan and add 2½ cups cold water. Cover tightly and bring to a boil over high heat. When you see steam beginning to escape, turn the heat down to very low, but do not remove the lid. Cook the rice over low heat for 20 minutes. Remove the pan from the heat but don't remove the lid. Let the rice stand, covered, for 20 minutes, then fluff with chopsticks and let cool completely. When cool, cover and refrigerate the rice overnight.

In a small mixing bowl, beat the eggs together with 2 tablespoons water. Rub a small, nonstick or well-seasoned skillet with some of the oil and place it over medium heat. Pour in enough egg to cover the bottom of the skillet, rotating the skillet to spread the egg mixture into a thin omelet. Cook until barely set. Turn and cook for a few seconds on the other side. Turn the omelet out onto a work surface and roll it up into a tube. Continue to make and roll up omelets until all of the egg mixture has been cooked. With a sharp knife, slice the rolls crosswise to make long, thin strips. Dice the pork and ham, and peel and cut the shrimp in half lengthwise; set aside.

Place a wok or large skillet over medium heat. Add the remaining oil and the garlic cloves. Cook, stirring, pressing down on the garlic to flavor the oil. When the garlic begins to brown, remove and discard it. Add the ginger and the cooked rice to the wok. Stir briefly, just so that the rice doesn't stick. Add the egg strips, diced meat, and shrimp and stir to combine them with the rice. Gradually stir in the chile-garlic sauce, if using, and the soy sauce. Add the green onions, stir once or twice, and sprinkle with the cilantro. Serve immediately.

SERVES 4 TO 6.

# Tortilla a la Española con Chorizo
## Spanish-Style Potato Omelet with Chorizo Sausage

¾ cup olive oil

1 pound red potatoes, peeled and thinly sliced

Coarse salt

1 large onion, peeled and thinly sliced

6 ounces Spanish chorizo, sliced

8 large eggs

Potatoes were brought to Spain from Ecuador in 1565 by explorer and conquistador Gonzalo Jimenez de Quesada. After it was discovered that sailors who ate potatoes during long voyages did not get scurvy, Basque sailors from northern Spain began to grow potatoes, and the tubers became a standard provision on Spanish ships. That is probably how the potato first reached Cuba.

In Spain, *tortilla* means "omelet," and the most classic and popular *tortilla* is made with potatoes and onions and sometimes chorizo. *Tortilla a la Española* is often served warm as a main course for lunch in Cuba.

If the idea of turning a half-cooked omelet out on a plate and slipping it back into the skillet makes you nervous, place the pan about five inches below the broiler (at low heat) and cook the tortilla until the top is firm.

In a well-seasoned, heavy 9- to 10-inch skillet, warm the oil over medium heat. Add some of the potato slices, one at a time so they don't stick together; season lightly with salt. Arrange some of the onion slices over the potatoes. Alternate layers of potatoes and onion, sprinkling each layer lightly with salt. Cook gently over medium to medium-low heat until the potatoes are tender but not browned and the onion is translucent, about 15 minutes.

Place a colander over a mixing bowl and drain the potato mixture, reserving the oil. Add the chorizo to the skillet and cook over medium heat until it begins to render its fat, about 2 minutes. Add the chorizo and drippings to the potato mixture. Wipe out the skillet, scraping off any stuck particles, as they will cause the omelet to stick.

In a large mixing bowl, beat the eggs, with salt to taste, until slightly foamy. Add the potatoes, onion, and chorizo and press them down with a spatula until completely covered with egg. Let the mixture settle for 15 minutes.

Pour ¼ cup of the reserved oil into the clean skillet and place over high heat. When the oil is very hot and has reached the smoking point, pour in the egg mixture, making sure that the potatoes, onion, and chorizo are evenly covered with egg. Lower the heat to medium, and shake the skillet gently back and forth to keep the eggs from sticking. When the eggs are firm, invert a plate over the skillet and carefully flip the omelet onto it. Slip the omelet back into the pan and continue to cook until set in the center. Turn the omelet out onto a platter. Cut into wedges and serve either hot or at room temperature.

SERVES 6 AS A MAIN COURSE OR 12 AS AN APPETIZER.

# Pato Yemayá
## Duck Yemayá

The Yoruba *orisha* (deity) Yemayá is the Lady of the Sea, and Mother of the Universe. The duck Kuekueye was her friend and confidant, but he betrayed Yemayá and was sentenced to be eaten as punishment for his treachery.

This interesting and delicious-sounding preparation of duck to honor Yemayá is described in a fascinating book called *Afro-Cuban Cuisine: Its Myths and Legends*, by Natalia Bolívar Aróstegui and Carmen González Díaz de Villegas. This is my interpretation of the dish they describe.

Remove the giblets and rinse the duck inside and out with cold water. With a sharp heavy knife, cut the duck into quarters.

In a nonreactive flameproof baking dish large enough to hold the duck pieces in a single layer, combine the bitter orange juice, onion, garlic, basil, ginger, cumin, marjoram, pepper, oil, and salt. Add the duck quarters and giblets, turning to coat them thoroughly with the marinade. Cover and marinate, refrigerated, for 2 to 3 hours. Remove the duck quarters and pat them dry with paper towels; reserve the marinade.

Preheat a charcoal grill to medium-hot and preheat the oven to 350° F.

Grill the duck, turning frequently, for 20 to 30 minutes, until crisp and browned. Place the duck, giblets, and marinade in the baking dish with enough *guarapo* to cover. Cover loosely with foil and bake in the oven for about 1 hour, until tender and cooked through. Remove the duck and skim the fat off the pan juices. Over high heat, boil the pan juices until most of the liquid evaporates, 10 to 15 minutes. Return the duck to the pan and turn to glaze the pieces with the pan juices.

SERVES 4.

1 large (6-pound) duck

½ cup bitter orange juice, or ¼ cup regular orange juice and ¼ cup fresh lime juice

⅓ cup thinly sliced onion

2 cloves garlic, crushed in a garlic press

1 tablespoon minced fresh basil, or ¾ teaspoon dried basil

1 tablespoon minced fresh ginger, or ¾ teaspoon dried ginger

½ teaspoon ground cumin

½ teaspoon marjoram

¼ teaspoon freshly ground black pepper (optional)

1 tablespoon olive oil

¼ teaspoon salt

About 2 (11.8-ounce) cans *guarapo* (sugarcane juice), or 1 cup sugar dissolved in 2 cups water

# Pargo a la Parilla Ciboney con Salsa de Aguacate
## Ciboney-Style Red Snapper with Avocado Sauce

Jorge (WaGaNXé) Salt and his wife, Tamara (aNoN), were born in Cuba and came to the United States as small children. They met and married in Florida and have two sons, Christopher (JaKiMil) and Christian (JiKi). The Salts are part of a growing Cuban-American Ciboney community in south Florida.

The grilled red snapper recipe that follows came from Jorge's grandmother Juana Parada Taxis, who lived near the city of Santiago de Cuba. Fish is a very important food for the Ciboney, and *waganache* (red tail snapper) is a favorite. Serve this dish with *Pan de Cazabé* (Modern Cassava [Yuca] Bread; page 37).

1 whole (4- to 4½-pound) red snapper, cleaned and scaled
Olive oil
Sea salt
1 lime, thinly sliced
1 small onion, thinly sliced
2 or 3 sprigs cilantro or *culantro*
*Salsa de Aguacate* (recipe follows)

Preheat a charcoal grill to medium-hot.

With a sharp knife, make 3 cuts diagonally down to the bone along each side of the fish. Rub the fish inside and out with oil and salt. Place the lime and onion slices and sprigs of cilantro in the cavity. Place the fish in a grill basket. Grill for 10 to 15 minutes on each side, or until the fish flakes when the flesh in one of the cuts is pierced with a fork. Place the fish on a platter and serve with the *Salsa de Aguacate*.

SERVES 4 TO 6.

# Salsa de Aguacate | Avocado Sauce

Using a fork, mash the avocado together with the lime juice. Stir in the olives, capers, and oil. Season with salt and pepper.

MAKES ABOUT 2 CUPS.

2 large, ripe Florida avocados, or 3 or 4 Hass avocados
2 to 4 tablespoons fresh lime juice, or to taste (from ½ to 1 lime)
½ cup drained pimiento-stuffed olives, sliced or chopped
1 tablespoon brine-packed capers, drained
6 tablespoons olive oil
Salt to taste
Freshly ground black pepper to taste (optional)

# Puerco con Arroz Amarillo y Quimbombó
## Pork with Yellow Rice and Okra

1/3 cup fresh lime juice

4 to 6 cloves garlic, peeled and lightly
  crushed but left whole

1 teaspoon salt, or to taste

2 pounds lean pork, cut into 1-inch cubes

Vegetable oil for deep-frying (optional)

1/4 cup olive oil

1 1/2 cups chopped bell pepper, preferably
  1/2 cup each green, yellow, and red

1 cup chopped onion

1 cup fresh or canned diced tomatoes,
  with their juices

1/2 teaspoon *bijol* (annatto seed
  seasoning)

1/3 pound fresh or frozen okra

1 cup Valencia or Arborio rice

2 2/3 cups chicken broth or water

Freshly ground black pepper to taste
  (optional)

1/2 teaspoon *Salsa Picante de Don Justo*
  (Don Justo's Hot Sauce; page 51) or
  other hot sauce to taste (optional)

Okra was first brought to Cuba by African slaves. On Cuban sugar plantations in the seventeenth century the cooks were usually African. These skillful women and men combined foods they were familiar with, like okra and plantains, with Spanish and Native American ingredients. This was the beginning of what would become Cuban creole cuisine.

Serve the pork with hot crusty *Pan Cubano* (Cuban Bread; page 95).

❖ ❖ ❖

In a large bowl, combine the lime juice, garlic, and salt. Add the pork and toss to coat it with the seasonings. Cover and marinate, refrigerated, for 1 to 3 hours, stirring occasionally. Remove the pork and garlic from the marinade with a slotted spoon and drain on paper towels. Reserve the marinade.

If deep-frying the pork, heat at least 2 inches of vegetable oil in a deep-fryer or deep, heavy skillet to 365° F. Add the pork in small batches and fry until golden brown, 2 to 3 minutes. Drain on paper towels and set aside.

If sautéing the pork, heat the olive oil in a large, heavy Dutch oven over medium-high heat. Add the pork in small batches and sauté until browned on all sides, 6 to 8 minutes. Do not crowd the pan or the meat won't brown properly. As the meat is browned, remove it with a slotted spoon and set aside.

If you deep-fried the pork, heat the olive oil in a large, heavy Dutch oven. If the pork was sautéed, continue to cook in the oil and drippings left in the Dutch oven. Add the bell peppers and onion and sauté over medium heat until the onion is translucent, about 5 minutes. Press or mince the reserved garlic and add it along with the reserved marinade, the tomatoes and their juice, and the *bijol*. Stir gently and continue to cook for 2 to 3 minutes.

If using fresh okra, trim off the ends and slice the pods into 1/2-inch-thick rounds. If using frozen okra, do not thaw.

Add the rice and okra to the sautéed vegetables and stir in the broth. Bring to a boil over high heat. Reduce the heat to low, cover, and simmer for 15 minutes. Add the pork and continue to simmer for 10 to 15 minutes, until the rice is tender and the pork is heated through. Taste and add salt, pepper, and hot sauce, if using. Serve hot.

SERVES 6 GENEROUSLY.

# Chilindrón de Carnero
## Lamb Stew

2 to 2½ pounds boneless lamb or kid
    shoulder, cut into 2-inch cubes; or
    3 to 3½ pounds lamb shanks or kid
    shanks

¼ cup fresh lime juice (from 1 large lime)

1½ to 2 tablespoons minced garlic
    (3 to 6 cloves)

1 to 2 *ajis cachucha*, seeded and minced;
    or ½ to 1 red jalapeño, seeded and
    minced

1 teaspoon ground cumin

½ teaspoon dried oregano leaves,
    crumbled

¼ to ½ teaspoon hot paprika, or to
    taste

Salt to taste

1 bay leaf (optional)

¾ cup flour

½ cup olive oil

1 large yellow onion, peeled and thinly
    sliced

1 green bell pepper, seeded and diced

1 (15-ounce) can diced tomatoes in juice

1 cup *vino seco* (Cuban dry cooking wine)
    or white wine

2 to 3 teaspoons brown sugar, or to
    taste

Freshly ground black pepper to taste
    (optional)

½ cup Spanish green olives stuffed with
    pimiento, sliced

¼ cup minced fresh parsley

In the small fishing village of Santa Fe on the outskirts of Havana, the Pacheco family has a simple *paladar* (a private restaurant) in the garden of their house overlooking the sea. Our friend Susana, who is a great cook herself, and her charming son George took us to this special place.

The menu depends on what fish was freshly caught that morning and what meats, raised by the family and neighbors, are available. All of the dishes are prepared with vegetables and herbs gathered fresh from the garden. To begin, we ate small red snapper, fried very simply and gently in oil until the skin was crisp and golden, and a salad of cucumbers, tomatoes, sliced onions, and lettuce. Then came a large platter of *chilindrón*, a spicy dish that may be made either with lamb or kid.

Kid especially is associated with the Afro-Cuban cooking and culture of the island. A peppery *chilindrón* of kid is a dish that might please Changó, the Santería *orisha* (deity) of Thunder, the Drums, and Dance. Serve the stew with *Pan de Cazabé* (Modern Cassava [Yuca] Bread; page 37), or with boiled potatoes or white rice.

Place the lamb in a large nonreactive baking dish or bowl. Add the lime juice, garlic, chiles, cumin, oregano, paprika, salt, and bay leaf, if using. Turn the lamb to coat it with the seasonings. Cover and refrigerate for at least 2 hours or overnight.

Preheat the oven to 325° F. Remove the lamb from the marinade and pat it dry with paper towels. Reserve the marinade. Dredge the lamb pieces in the flour, shaking off any excess. In a large, heavy Dutch oven over medium heat, heat the oil. Brown the lamb in batches, without allowing the pieces to touch. As the pieces are browned, remove them with a slotted spoon and set aside.

Add the onion and bell pepper to the pan and sauté over medium heat until slightly softened, about 5 minutes. Add the tomatoes, wine, reserved marinade, and brown sugar, stirring to incorporate any browned pan juices. Return the lamb to the pot and bring to a simmer on top of the stove. Cover and cook in the oven for about 1½ hours, until the lamb is very tender. Stir, taste, and correct the seasonings, adding more salt and pepper, if needed. Remove and discard the bay leaf. Stir in the olives and parsley and serve.

SERVES 6.

# Pudín de Mamey
## Mamey Pudding

Spanish settlers arriving in Cuba were delighted to find tropical fruits like guava and mamey growing wild on the island. They soon adapted recipes brought from Seville or Madrid to include these delicious new foods. Puddings and flans are classic Spanish desserts. In this recipe, the addition of pureed fresh mamey gives the pudding a lovely pink-orange color and delicate fruit flavor. As a variation, instead of buttering the mold, line it with a pale golden caramel, as in the recipe for *Flan de Leche Clásico* (Classic Flan; page 92).

Preheat the oven to 350° F. Butter a 5½-inch charlotte mold, a 4- to 6-cup soufflé dish, or a metal ring mold.

If using a fresh mamey, use a sharp paring knife to remove the thin brown skin and large pits. Press the mamey flesh through a coarse sieve into a bowl; you should have about 1½ cups puree. Whisk in the eggs, sweetened condensed milk, vanilla, cinnamon, and salt. Pour the mixture into the prepared mold. Place the mold in a larger baking pan and pour in enough boiling water to come halfway up the sides. Bake on the middle rack of the oven until it is slightly firm to the touch and a toothpick inserted in the center comes out clean, about 40 minutes. Remove the mold from the water bath and allow to cool on a rack. Cover and refrigerate, until chilled, at least 2 hours. Run a thin-bladed knife around the edges of the pudding and invert it onto a serving plate. Decorate the pudding with swirls of whipped cream and garnish with mint leaves or toasted shredded coconut.

**SERVES 4 TO 6.**

2 teaspoons butter

1 ripe medium-size red mamey sapote, or 1½ cups fresh or frozen mamey puree

2 large eggs, beaten

½ cup sweetened condensed milk

½ teaspoon pure vanilla extract

½ teaspoon ground cinnamon

Pinch of salt

Lightly sweetened whipped cream

Fresh mint leaves or toasted shredded coconut

# Tocino de Cielo
## Egg Custard from Heaven

**FOR THE CARAMEL**
½ cup sugar

**FOR THE CUSTARD**
12 large egg yolks
2 cups sugar
½ vanilla bean, or ½ teaspoon pure
   vanilla extract

*Tocino de cielo* is an old Cuban dessert custard with deep roots in Andalucia. It is a specialty of Jerez de la Frontera, where egg whites were traditionally used to clarify sherry before it was bottled. Making this amazingly rich custard was originally a delicious way to use up the leftover yolks.

This is how my friend Virginia Flores-Godoy remembers being introduced to this heavenly dessert: "My great-grandfather Don Ramón Flores de Apodaca was an officer in the Spanish Royal Navy who came to Havana from Cadiz in the late 1800s. He brought with him a taste for the delicacies of his native Andalusia. Sunday lunches at my paternal grandparents' home were long and exquisitely interpreted by Rafael, their Cantonese cook. After a menu of gazpacho, red snapper, and filet mignon, we were offered a wide array of desserts—sumptuous *tocinos de cielo*, *coquimol*, *yemas dobles*, and other confections made with eggs and sugar."

This recipe describes the traditional Cuban method of caramelizing a mold; for an alternate—and perhaps easier—technique, see the instructions in the recipe for *Flan de Leche Clásico* (Classic Flan) on page 92.

Make the caramel: Place the sugar in a 4-cup metal charlotte mold or a shallow 8-inch round or square metal cake pan. Place the mold directly on the burner over medium heat. Using oven mitts to protect your hands, turn and tip the mold over the heat until the sugar melts and turns a pale amber. Remove the mold from the heat and tip it so that the hot caramel coats the bottom and part of the sides evenly. Set aside.

Make the custard: Place the egg yolks and 2 tablespoons cold water in a mixing bowl and whisk until combined but not foamy.

In a medium-size, heavy saucepan, combine the sugar and 1 cup plus 2 tablespoons water. Slit the vanilla bean down one side with a sharp knife and scrape the pulp of the bean into the syrup (or add the vanilla extract, if using). Cook for a few minutes at medium heat until the sugar dissolves and the syrup turns clear. Remove from the heat and set aside.

Gradually pour the hot syrup into the egg yolks, stirring constantly, until well combined. Pour the egg mixture through a coarse strainer into the still-warm, caramel-coated mold.

Place the lid on the charlotte mold or cover the top with aluminum foil.

Fill the bottom of a tall stock pot fitted with a steamer basket with enough hot water to almost reach the basket. Place the mold in the basket and cover the pot tightly with a lid. Steam the custard over simmering water for 45 to 55 minutes, until the custard seems fairly firm, and a toothpick inserted in the center comes out almost clean. Check the water level occasionally and, if needed, add additional hot water, making sure that it doesn't get into the mold. Remove the mold, take off the lid or foil, and let the custard cool, then refrigerate it, loosely covered, for several hours or overnight.

To serve, run a thin-bladed knife around the edge of the custard. Place a serving plate face down on top of the mold. Gripping the mold and plate together with both hands, invert the custard onto the plate. Slice and serve with the caramel from the mold.

SERVES 8 TO 10.

# Sorbete de Mango y Jengibre
## Mango and Ginger Sorbet

1½ cups sugar

1 rounded teaspoon finely grated lime zest

¾ teaspoon ground ginger

1 tablespoon unflavored gelatin

3 cups pureed fresh mango (from 2 to 4 ripe mangoes)

3 tablespoons fresh lime juice

Chinese immigrants from the United States started the first ice cream stands in Cuba. This doesn't seem strange when you consider that the Chinese are credited with the invention of fruit ices, but it was an American invention, the crank ice cream machine, patented in 1847, that revolutionized ice cream making. Between 1860 and 1875, thousands of Chinese who had come to California as miners and railroad builders immigrated to Cuba to escape discrimination caused by the Chinese Exclusion Act. Among them were some entrepreneurial individuals who thought ice cream stands could be a lucrative business. They hit the jackpot: Cubans developed a passion for ice cream that continues to this day.

In a medium saucepan, combine 1½ cups water with the sugar, lime zest, and ginger. Cook over medium heat, stirring occasionally, until the sugar is dissolved and the syrup turns clear, about 5 minutes. Remove from the heat and set aside.

In a small bowl, sprinkle the gelatin over ¼ cup cold water and let it stand for 1 minute to soften. Add the gelatin to the hot syrup and stir until dissolved.

In a mixing bowl, combine the mango puree and lime juice. Pour the syrup through a fine-mesh sieve into the puree and stir to combine. Chill the mango mixture for about 30 minutes, then pour into an ice cream maker and freeze according to the manufacturer's directions.

If you don't have an ice cream maker, pour the sorbet mixture into a stainless-steel mixing bowl and place it in the freezer. When the mixture begins to harden, beat, using an electric mixer set at medium speed or a whisk, until it is light and fluffy. Return it to the freezer. Repeat this process 2 or 3 times, or until the frozen mixure has a light, smooth, less icy texture.

**MAKES 6 TO 8 CUPS; SERVES 8.**

# Sandia Ochumare
## Watermelon Ochumare

In their facinating book *Afro-Cuban Cuisine: Its Myths and Legends*, Natalia Bolívar Aróstegui and Carmen González Días de Villegas describe this festive and refreshing dessert as part of a menu to please Yemayá, the Yoruba *orisha* of the sea and mother of the universe.

❖ ❖ ❖

Cut off the top of the melon for a lid. With a sharp knife and a large spoon, hollow out the watermelon, removing chunks large enough to dice into bite-size pieces, reserving any juice. Dice the melon flesh and set it aside in a large bowl. Pour the juice from the melon through a strainer into a large measuring cup. To 1 cup watermelon juice, add the *guarapo*, *aguardiente*, and lime juice. Peel and dice the pineapple, and peel and slice the orange into rounds. Add the pineapple, orange, and grapes to the melon in the bowl. Gently spoon the fruit back into the melon shell and carefully pour in the juice mixture. Put on the lid and chill the watermelon until very cold. Serve, garnished with mint.

SERVES 4 TO 6.

1 small round seedless watermelon
½ cup *guarapo* (sugarcane juice), or
   ¼ cup sugar dissolved in ½ cup water
½ cup *aguardiente* or light rum
1 fresh pineapple
2 oranges
1 cup seedless grapes, halved (optional)
2 tablespoons fresh lime juice
Fresh mint

# Churros
## Spanish Doughnuts

1 cup milk
1 tablespoon butter
1 teaspoon salt
2 cups flour, sifted
1 teaspoon pure vanilla extract (optional)
Vegetable oil for deep-frying
Sugar or cinnamon sugar for dusting

There is no snack more traditionally Spanish than *churros*, crisp doughnut sticks or loops, sprinkled with sugar and consumed with a cup of rich, thick hot chocolate. Both *churros* and the technique of deep-frying were first brought to Cuba by the Spanish. Today, hundreds of years later, Cubans are still deep-frying *churros*—and everything else, from pork to plantains.

In a heavy-bottomed saucepan, combine the milk, 1 cup water, the butter, and salt and bring to a boil over medium-high heat. Remove from the heat and quickly mix in the flour and vanilla, if using, with a wooden spatula, stirring vigorously until the mixture comes away from the sides of the pan. Set the dough aside to cool to room temperature.

In a deep-fryer or a large, deep, heavy-bottomed skillet, heat at least 2 inches of oil to 400° F. Fill a *churro* press or a cookie press fitted with a large ribbon or star tip with the dough. Press out the dough in 4-inch lengths and let it drop into the hot oil. Fry, turning once with a slotted spoon, until golden, 2 to 3 minutes. Fry only 2 or 3 *churros* at a time to avoid lowering the oil temperature. Remove the *churros* from the oil, drain them on paper towels, and roll in sugar. Serve warm.

MAKES ABOUT 15 *CHURROS*; SERVES 4 TO 6.

# Pan de Cazabé
## Modern Cassava (Yuca) Bread

Yuca, also called yucca, cassava, or manioc, has always been the most important crop for the Ciboney and Taino peoples of Cuba. There are two basic varieties, bitter yuca (which is not generally available in the United States) and sweet yuca. The bitter variety contains a high level of prussic acid and is toxic if not properly prepared: It must be completely peeled, then the white flesh grated and all of the toxic juices pressed out. The Ciboney and Taino dipped the points of their arrows in this poisonous liquid, and the flesh was then dried, pounded into flour, and made into unleavened crackerlike bread called *cazabé*. Sweet yuca, the kind found fresh in supermarket produce departments, must also be carefully peeled and boiled before eating, but is not highly toxic. Sweet yuca has a texture and flavor similar to that of a potato (and indeed russet potatoes can be used in place of yuca in this recipe).

Not many people these days prepare traditional *cazabé* at home, though it is made commercially and sold at Cuban and Latin American grocery stores in the United States. The pizzalike bread that follows, made with cooked sweet yuca, is a tasty modern variation.

Peel the yuca with a vegetable peeler, making sure to remove both the waxed outer peel and the rosy underpeel. This may also be done with a paring knife: Insert the tip of the knife under the peel and underpeel to loosen them, then use your hands to peel them off. Cut the white flesh crosswise into 2 or 3 pieces. Cook it in a large pot of unsalted boiling water until the pieces begin to split open, about 20 minutes. Add ¼ cup cold water and continue to cook for an additional 5 to 10 minutes, until tender when pierced with a knife. Remove the yuca with a slotted spoon and remove and discard the fibrous core. Using the coarse side of a box grater, grate the cooked yuca. (If substituting potatoes, peel, boil until tender, then grate.)

Preheat the oven to 450° F. Place a pizza stone or griddle in the oven to preheat.

In a large mixing bowl, combine the flour, baking powder, and salt. Make a well in the flour mixture. In a large measuring cup, stir together 1 cup of the grated yuca, the eggs, oil, and ¼ cup water. Pour this mixture into the well in the flour. Stir with a wooden spoon until the dough comes together, adding a little extra water if the dough seems dry. Knead on a lightly floured work surface until smooth and elastic, 3 to 5 minutes.

Roll out the dough to fit the pizza stone, about ½ inch thick. Prick in several places with a fork. Bake for 8 to 10 minutes, until golden. Cut the bread into wedges and serve.

SERVES 4 TO 6.

1 pound small, firm yuca (cassava)
2½ cups all-purpose flour, plus more for dusting work surface
2½ teaspoons baking powder
1 teaspoon salt
2 large eggs
½ cup olive oil

# TWO | Clásicos Criollas ▣ Creole Classics

# Clásicos Criollas | Creole Classics

Since the late 1400s, the foods and flavors of Cuba's original Ciboney and Taino inhabitants have simmered along with those of Spanish conquistadors, African slaves, Chinese coolies from the gold fields of California, native Yucatecans, French and African settlers from Haiti, the Dominican Republic, and Jamaica, immigrants from mainland China, and assorted Europeans to produce the international *fricasé* that became Cuban creole cuisine. After the Spanish-American war in 1898, food traditions from the United States also added their spice to the pot. Though all of these cultures have contributed, the strongest single culinary influence in Cuba is Spain. Unlike the cooking of other Caribbean islands, most Cuban cooking, though well seasoned, is far from fiery. Hot chiles are not popular; in fact, traditional Cuban cooks seldom reach for the pepper grinder. As in Spain, garlic, onion, olive oil, oregano, cumin, and salt are widely used in savory dishes, and cinnamon, nutmeg, vanilla, and citrus zest are prominent in desserts. However, the addition of cilantro, *culantro*, bitter orange juice, and lime juice in marinades and the inclusion of Caribbean and African vegetables such as yuca, *boniato*, and okra give Cuban dishes their own distinctive identity.

To go food shopping in modern Cuba, you'd best be quick and nimble. No one leaves the house without stuffing a plastic grocery bag in his or her pocket. Eggs, for example, are often hard to come by. Officially they are rationed, and making an old-fashioned egg-rich dessert like *Tocino de Cielo* (page 32) would use up the egg allowance of a family of four for one month. That was what made one experience Marty and I had in Havana even more interesting. One day while walking near our hotel, we noticed people streaming out of a local bodega carrying not just one or two dozen eggs, but three or four flats of them. As other people spotted the egg carriers they also headed for the bodega. That, we were told, is how shopping is done in Cuba. Whether it is eggs or cabbages, you have to be alert and ready to stock up. Once you have whatever it is, you can barter for other necessities with someone who stocked up

on milk, mangoes, or coffee. For this reason, it is often both difficult and expensive for cooks in Cuba to assemble the ingredients necessary to prepare traditional creole dishes. As a cook, I always appreciate when friends invite me to their home for dinner, because I realize how much work is involved. People we met in Cuba were invariably kind and generous. Though they were far too gracious to even hint that entertaining us required considerable effort, we knew that it did, and will never forget their hospitality and the good food and fellowship shared at their tables.

# Aceite de Achiote
## Achiote-Flavored Olive Oil

1 cup olive oil
¼ cup achiote seeds
1 small fresh or dried hot chile (optional)

Achiote, also called annatto, is used throughout the Caribbean and Latin America as a coloring and flavoring for food. The small, hard, brick-red seeds grow in clusters on *Bixa orellana*, a flowering tropical tree. In Cuban cooking, the whole seeds are used to color and flavor cooking oil, and ground seeds are combined with cumin and corn flour to make *bijol*, a seasoning that is often substituted for more expensive saffron. I have used achiote in cooking for many years, but the first time I actually saw it growing was at the Jardín Botánico Nacional on the outskirts of Havana. Achiote oil adds both a lovely golden color and subtle but unique flavor to Cuban dishes like *arroz con pollo* and *ropa vieja*. If you like spicier food, add a small hot chile to the oil. When stored in the refrigerator, achiote oil will last for several months.

In a small saucepan, warm the oil over low heat. Add the achiote seeds and the chile, if using. Simmer, stirring occasionally, for about 5 minutes, until the oil turns a rich orange color. Remove the oil from the heat and let it cool. Pour the oil through a strainer into a small jar. Discard the seeds and chile.

**MAKES 1 CUP.**

# Arroz Blanco
## White Rice

**R**ice is served at least once a day in most Cuban households. Except for dishes like *arroz con pollo* and *arroz con leche*, where the creamier texture of short-grain rice is desirable, Cubans usually prefer to cook with long-grain rice. The best recipe I have ever found for perfect, fluffy white rice is the one included by Mary Urrutia Randelman in her excellent cookbook and fascinating culinary memoir, *Memories of a Cuban Kitchen*. Randelman's method is simple, relatively fool-proof, and, as she notes, completely different from the package instructions. The recipe that follows is adapted from hers.

2 cups raw long-grain or converted white rice

2 tablespoons olive oil

1 clove garlic, peeled and crushed (optional)

1½ to 2 teaspoons salt

4 cups water if using long-grain rice; 5 cups if using converted

Combine the rice, oil, garlic, salt, and water in a large saucepan and bring to a boil over high heat. Cook, uncovered, until most of the water has been absorbed and craters form on top of the rice, 10 to 15 minutes.

Stir the rice with a fork, cover the pan, and reduce the heat to low. Cook for an additional 8 to 10 minutes, until the rice is fluffy. Fluff the rice with a fork and serve immediately.

MAKES 3 CUPS.

# Caldo de Res
## Beef Broth

2 pounds beef bones, shin bones if possible

4 cloves garlic, crushed in a garlic press

2 teaspoons salt

¾ teaspoon ground cumin

½ teaspoon *bijol* (annatto seed seasoning; optional)

½ teaspoon dried oregano leaves, preferably Mexican oregano

1 large onion, peeled and halved

1 large green bell pepper, seeded and halved

1½ pounds flank steak

6 plum tomatoes, quartered

1 bay leaf

Beef broth is the base for traditional Cuban dishes like *ajiaco* and *ropa vieja*. Though some home cooks skip the step of browning the beef bones and vegetables, chefs like our friend Eduardo know that browning gives this broth a deep amber color and rich, full flavor. This recipe also yields the beef for *Ropa Vieja de Raquel* (Raquel's Shredded Beef; page 77).

Preheat the oven to 350° F. Place the beef bones in a shallow roasting pan and brown in the oven for 30 minutes. While the bones are roasting, mash the garlic together with the salt, cumin, *bijol*, if using, and oregano and set aside. After 15 minutes, add the onion and bell pepper to the roasting pan and continue to roast for the remaining 15 minutes, until lightly browned. With tongs, remove the bones and roasted vegetables to a 3- to 4-gallon soup pot. Add the flank steak, tomatoes, bay leaf, garlic mixture, and 3 quarts water.

Cover and bring the water to a boil over medium-high heat. Uncover the pot and skim off any scum that has risen to the top. Reduce the heat to low. Simmer the broth with the lid slightly askew until the meat is very tender, 1½ to 2 hours.

Strain the broth through a colander lined with two layers of damp cheesecloth. Remove the flank steak and reserve for *Ropa Vieja de Raquel*.

Discard the remaining solids. Refrigerate the broth; when chilled, skim off any fat from the top.

MAKES 2½ QUARTS.

# Frijoles Negros
## Classic Cuban-Style Black Beans

**B**lack beans are a cornerstone of Cuban cooking. Served with fluffy white rice, they are the perfect accompaniment for meat, fish, or poultry. They can also stand alone as a nourishing entrée or be pureed to make another Cuban classic, black bean soup.

The cooking time will depend both on the dryness of the beans and the altitude. At sea level they may be cooked in an hour, but at high altitudes it may take two to three hours. For that reason, many high-altitude bean cooks prefer to use the pressure cooker method discussed in the Glossary (page 180).

Make the beans: Pick over the beans and rinse them under cold running water. Place the beans in a large nonreactive pot and add enough cold water to cover them by about 2 inches. Soak the beans overnight, or, for a quick soak, bring the beans and water to a boil, boil for 2 minutes, remove from the heat, cover the pot, and let soak for 1 hour.

After soaking, if needed add enough additional water to cover the beans by 2 inches. Add the bell pepper, garlic, and bay leaf to the pot and bring to a boil over medium-high heat.

Lower the heat and simmer, uncovered, stirring occasionally, until the beans are tender, 1 to 3 hours. If more water is needed during cooking, add hot water, as cold water tends to toughen the beans. Periodically skim off any foam that rises to the top of the pot.

While the beans are cooking, make the sofrito: In a large skillet over medium heat, warm the oil. Add the onion and bell pepper and sauté until the onion turns translucent, 3 to 4 minutes. Add the garlic, cumin, salt, pepper, and cinnamon and cook for 1 minute more, then remove from the heat.

Place 1 cup of the cooked beans and half of the sofrito in a blender or food processor and pulse until pureed. Stir the puree and the remaining sofrito into the pot of beans. Taste; add vinegar and sugar, if necessary, and, if you like, a drizzle of oil to complete the seasoning. Bring the beans to a boil again, then reduce the heat to low and simmer, uncovered, stirring frequently to avoid sticking, for about 10 minutes to blend the flavors.

SERVES 8 TO 10.

### FOR THE BEANS

1 (16-ounce) bag (2 cups) dried black beans

1 green bell pepper, seeded and quartered

2 cloves garlic, peeled and lightly crushed

1 bay leaf

### FOR THE SOFRITO

⅓ cup olive oil

1 large onion, peeled and finely chopped (about 2 cups)

1 green bell pepper, seeded and chopped (about 1 cup)

1 tablespoon minced garlic (3 to 4 cloves)

1½ to 2 teaspoons ground cumin, or to taste

1 teaspoon salt, or to taste

½ teaspoon freshly ground black pepper (optional)

¼ teaspoon ground cinnamon

1 to 2 tablespoons white distilled vinegar

1 to 2 tablespoons raw or brown sugar (optional)

Olive oil (optional)

# Mojo Criollo
## Cuban Garlic Sauce

½ to ¾ teaspoon whole cumin seeds, or
   to taste

¼ cup olive oil

1 teaspoon dried oregano leaves,
   crumbled

1 rosemary sprig or bay leaf

1 whole head garlic, cloves separated and
   peeled

1½ teaspoons salt

2 cups fresh bitter orange juice, or 1 cup
   regular orange juice and 1 cup fresh
   lime juice

This classic Cuban seasoning sauce is a wonderful marinade for meat, fish, poultry, and vegetables. Not only is Ana Menéndez an award-winning journalist and author, she is also a wonderful cook. In a fun and informative article Ana wrote about Cuban-American observances of Thanksgiving, she recalls that when she was a small child, "Roast pork was the centerpiece of the annual Thanksgiving meal celebrated by a Cuban immigrant family, bound together by common memories and hopes. As the years passed, the gatherings became smaller, culinary tastes changed, and turkey nudged the pig off the table." Whether preparing a whole fifty-pound pig or a small turkey, marinating the meat in *mojo* before roasting is essential. Every family has its own way of preparing *mojo criollo*. Ana has been kind enough to share her recipe with us. This amount of sauce is enough to marinate a whole turkey. If marinating a pig, double or triple the recipe.

Toast the cumin seeds in a dry skillet over medium heat until fragrant. Pound the seeds with a mortar and pestle and stir them into the oil, along with the oregano and rosemary. In the same mortar, crush the garlic and salt to make a smooth paste. To make that operation easier, you may want to crush the garlic in a garlic press first. In a saucepan over medium-low heat, heat the oil mixture until fragrant. Do not let it sizzle. Let the oil cool, then remove and discard the rosemary. Place the oil, garlic mixture, and bitter orange juice in a blender and blend well.

MAKES ABOUT 2¼ CUPS.

# Mojo Vinegreta
## *Mojo* Dip or Salad Dressing

This versatile dip or dressing is traditionally made in a mortar, the garlic ground into a paste with a pestle. I have found that a garlic press works well as an alternative and is an implement more cooks in the United States are apt to have in their kitchens.

Crush the garlic in a garlic press into a small mixing bowl and use a fork to mash it together with the salt to make a paste. Stir in the bitter orange juice, then gradually whisk in the oil. If preparing the *mojo* in advance, cover it tightly and store in the refrigerator. It will last for up to 1 week. If chilled, let the *mojo* come to room temperature before serving. For a warm dip or dressing, heat it gently in a small saucepan over low heat, whisking constantly.

**MAKES ABOUT 1 CUP.**

**2 to 3 cloves garlic**
**½ teaspoon salt**
**¼ cup fresh bitter orange juice, or**
　**2 tablespoons regular orange juice and**
　**2 tablespoons fresh lime juice**
**¾ cup extra-virgin olive oil**

# Salsa Española
## Spanish Sauce

½ cup olive oil

1½ cups chopped onion (1 medium)

1 cup chopped green bell pepper (1 small)

2 cups peeled, seeded, and diced fresh tomatoes, or 1 (14.5-ounce) can diced tomatoes in juice

1 (8-ounce) can tomato sauce

1 cup dry white wine

4 teaspoons minced garlic (2 to 3 cloves)

½ teaspoon dried oregano leaves, crumbled (optional)

½ teaspoon ground cumin (optional)

Salt to taste

2 to 3 tablespoons chopped fresh parsley, preferably flat-leaf parsley (optional)

Like *sofrito* and *mojo criollo*, this versatile tomato sauce is a base of Cuban creole cooking. It is an important ingredient in the *Ajíes Rellenos con Chorizo, Arroz, y Tomate* (Stuffed Peppers) recipe on page 71 and a delicious sauce to serve over eggs, meat, fish, chicken, or pasta. It is quick and easy enough to make as needed, but may be kept in the refrigerator for a few days or frozen for up to 1 month.

Place the oil in a large skillet over medium heat. Add the onion and bell pepper and sauté until the onion is translucent, about 5 minutes. Stir in the tomatoes, tomato sauce, wine, garlic, oregano and cumin, if using, and salt. Simmer the sauce gently for 10 to 15 minutes. Taste and adjust the seasonings. Stir in the parsley, if desired, and serve.

MAKES ABOUT 3 CUPS.

# Salsa Picante de Don Justo
## Don Justo's Hot Sauce

ood in Cuba's western provinces, like Spanish food, is well seasoned but almost never hot and spicy. *Cachuchas*, the hottest chiles found at farmers markets in Havana, resemble the fiery habaneros and Scotch bonnets popular on other Caribbean islands, but are surprisingly mild.

Don Justo, who has traveled the world as a ship's cook, grew up in Oriente, Cuba's easternmost province, where there is more Jamaican, Haitian, and Dominican influence in the cooking. At his small neighborhood *paladar* in Havana, he seasons the food to suit Havana palates, but keeps a bottle of homemade hot sauce in the pantry, to give fire eaters from the other side of the island a taste of home.

When handling hot chiles, it's a good idea to wear rubber gloves. Though it is usually not refrigerated in the Caribbean, I prefer to store this hot sauce in the refrigerator. Either way, it will keep indefinitely.

Wash and rinse a 12-ounce bottle thoroughly. As an added precaution, I sometimes run it through the dishwasher without soap.

Place the chiles in a colander and rinse under cool running water. Drain thoroughly, and remove the stems. Place the chiles and garlic in the bottle. In a small saucepan over medium heat, bring the vinegar, salt, and sugar just to a simmer, stirring to dissolve the salt and sugar. Using a funnel, pour the vinegar mixture into the bottle and set aside to cool thoroughly. When cool, close the bottle with a cork or other nonreactive top and store it in the refrigerator. The sauce will be ready in a few days, but will get hotter as it sits. Until the peppers lose their heat, just top up the bottle with vinegar, or even a little rum, as needed.

MAKES 1 (12-OUNCE) BOTTLE

**A handful of fresh or dried small hot red chiles**

**3 or 4 garlic cloves, peeled and halved lengthwise**

**1 to 1½ cups distilled white vinegar or cider vinegar**

**1 teaspoon salt**

**1 teaspoon sugar**

# Ajiaco Moderno
## Modern Meat and Vegetable Stew

**FOR THE BROTH**

½ pound dry-cured smoked Spanish chorizo, or ½ pound fresh Mexican-style chorizo

1 pound pork loin or shoulder

6 chicken thighs, bone in

2 tablespoons olive oil

4 cups *Caldo de Res* (Beef Broth; page 46)

4 cups chicken broth

2 bay leaves

**FOR THE SOFRITO**

¼ cup olive oil

2 cups chopped onion

2 cups chopped green bell pepper

1 rounded tablespoon minced garlic

2 teaspoons ground cumin

1 (14.5-ounce) can diced tomatoes in rich juice or puree

**FOR THE STEW**

1 cup each of *ñame* (African yam), yellow *malanga* (yellow taro root), *boniato* (white sweet potato), and yuca

1 green plantain

¼ cup fresh lime juice

1 cup calabaza or butternut squash

3 to 4 ears fresh sweet corn

1 ripe plantain

Salt to taste

3 to 4 tablespoons minced fresh cilantro

*Salsa Picante de Don Justo* (Don Justo's Hot Sauce; page 51) to taste (optional)

There are almost as many variations on *ajiaco* as there are Cuban cooks. The traditional base of this hearty soup or stew is root vegetables, cooked with whatever meat is available. This version includes pork and chicken, the two meats that are most available in modern Cuba. Serve the *ajiaco* with warm, crusty *Pan Cubano* (Cuban Bread; page 95).

Make the broth: With a sharp knife, cut the chorizo into 1-inch lengths. Cut the pork into 1½-inch pieces. Remove and discard the skin and excess fat from the chicken thighs. In a large sauté pan or deep skillet over medium heat, heat the oil. Add the chorizo and cook until lightly browned on all sides, 4 to 5 minutes. Remove the chorizo with a slotted spoon and set aside. Brown the pork and then the chicken in the chorizo drippings for 8 to 10 minutes total. Place the chorizo, beef, and chicken in a large Dutch oven and add the beef and chicken broths, 4 cups water, and the bay leaves. Bring to a boil over high heat, then reduce the heat to low. Cover and simmer for 15 minutes.

Meanwhile, make the sofrito: In the skillet, over medium heat, heat the oil. Add the onion and bell pepper, reduce the heat to medium-low, and cook, stirring often, until the onion is softened, 8 to 10 minutes. Stir in the garlic, cumin, and tomatoes and continue to simmer gently for 6 to 8 minutes.

Add the sofrito to the meats and broth and simmer for 15 minutes.

Make the stew: Peel and cube the *ñame*, *malanga*, *boniato*, and yuca, placing them in a bowl of cold water as you work so they don't discolor. Peel the green plantain and cut it into ½-inch-thick slices; toss the green plantain with the lime juice.

Drain the root vegetables and add them to the stew. Reserving the lime juice, drain the green plantain and add it to the stew. Return the stew to a boil over high heat, then reduce the heat to low, cover, and continue to simmer for 20 minutes. Peel and cube the calabaza, add and simmer for 15 minutes. Cut the corn into 2-inch lengths, add and simmer for an additional 10 minutes. Cut the ripe plantain into 1-inch lengths. Toss it with the reserved lime juice and cook it separately in a saucepan of boiling water until tender when pierced with a knife. Peel the ripe plantain pieces and add them to the stew. Season with salt and simmer for 10 to 15 minutes to blend the flavors. Sprinkle in the cilantro and spoon the stew into soup bowls. Serve with *Salsa Picante de Don Justo*.

**SERVES 6 TO 8 GENEROUSLY.**

# Puerco Asado
## Roast Pork Loin

Traditionally, a whole roast suckling pig is served for family gatherings on *Nochebuena* (Christmas Eve), but for today's smaller families, a roast loin of pork prepared in the same traditional way is just as festive and a bit more manageable.

Pierce the roast all over with the tip of sharp paring knife to a depth of about ½ inch to allow the seasonings to penetrate the meat.

Crush the garlic in a garlic press into a small mixing bowl. Add the salt, oregano, cumin, and pepper and mash together with fork to make a paste. Place the roast in a nonreactive baking dish. Rub the roast well with the paste and add the bitter orange juice and ½ cup sherry. Sprinkle the onion rings over the top. Cover with plastic wrap and marinate, refrigerated, for at least 4 hours or preferably overnight. Turn the roast once or twice while marinating.

When ready to roast, preheat the oven to 400° F. Remove the roast from the marinade and pat dry; reserve the marinade and onion. Place it in a Dutch oven or roasting pan just large enough to hold it comfortably. Roast for 20 minutes, then lower the oven temperature to 325° F. and add the marinade and onion. Continue to cook, basting every 15 minutes with the pan juices, until the pork reaches an internal temperature of 175° F., 40 to 50 minutes. If the pan juices begin to dry up, add up to ½ cup additional sherry and a little water, if needed. Remove the roast from the oven and let it rest, loosely covered with foil, for 10 to 15 minutes.

Meanwhile, add 1 cup water to the roasting pan and stir to loosen any browned bits. Bring to a boil on top of the stove and cook, stirring, until the juices have reduced to about ½ cup. Slice the pork thinly and serve it with the onion and pan sauce. For a richer pan sauce, swirl the butter into the juices just before serving.

SERVES 4 TO 6.

1 (2½- to 3-pound) boneless center-cut pork loin roast

6 cloves garlic, peeled

1 tablespoon salt

1 teaspoon dried oregano leaves

½ teaspoon ground cumin

¼ teaspoon freshly ground black pepper (optional)

½ cup fresh bitter orange juice, or ¼ cup regular orange and ¼ cup fresh lime juice

½ to 1 cup dry sherry or dry white wine

1 large onion, sliced into thick rings

1 tablespoon butter (optional)

# Potaje de Frijoles Colorados
## Red Bean Soup

1 cup diced thick-sliced bacon (4 ounces)

1 cup diced chorizo or ham steak

¼ cup olive oil

1½ cups chopped onion (1 medium)

1½ cups chopped Anaheim chiles or
   green bell pepper

3 to 4 cloves garlic

1 teaspoon salt

1 teaspoon ground cumin

½ teaspoon dried oregano leaves

¼ teaspoon freshly ground black pepper
   (optional)

3 to 4 cups cooked red beans

1 (15-ounce) can diced tomatoes in juice

4 cups chicken broth

½ cup white wine

Juice of 1 lime (about 2 tablespoons)

1 cup peeled diced red potato (1 medium)

1 cup peeled diced calabaza or butternut
   squash

2 to 4 tablespoons minced fresh cilantro
   or flat-leaf parsley (optional)

The beans most often associated with Cuban cooking are *frijoles negros*, but Cubans eat many kinds of beans and legumes. Red beans are especially popular in the eastern provinces, where they are used to make *congrí* (red beans and rice), and hearty soups like this one. Serve with crusty *Pan Cubano* (Cuban Bread; page 95).

In a large skillet, cook the bacon over medium-low heat until crisp, 8 to 10 minutes.

With a slotted spoon, remove the bacon and place it in a Dutch oven or large saucepan. To the skillet, add the chorizo and cook, stirring often, for 5 minutes. Remove it with the slotted spoon and add it to the bacon. Pour off all but a thin film of drippings from the skillet. Add the onion and chiles to the skillet and cook over medium-low heat, stirring, until translucent, 3 to 5 minutes. While the onion mixture is cooking, crush the garlic in a garlic press into a mortar or small bowl. Add the salt, cumin, oregano, and black pepper and use a pestle or a fork to mash the seasonings to a paste. Add the seasonings to the onion mixture and cook, stirring, for 1 minute. Add this sofrito to the meats. Stir in the beans, tomatoes, broth, wine, and lime juice. Bring the soup to a boil over high heat. Add the potato and calabaza. Cover, reduce the heat to low, and simmer for about 20 minutes, or until the vegetables are tender. Sprinkle the soup with the cilantro, if desired, and serve.

SERVES 6 GENEROUSLY.

# Puré de Frijoles Negros Ràpido
## Quick Black Bean Soup

Though it calls for canned black beans, this easy soup has a great old-fashioned flavor. The secret, according to my friend Virginia Flores-Godoy, is to take the time to cook your sofrito slowly so that the flavors blend.

In a large saucepan over medium heat, heat the oil. Add the chorizo and sauté until very lightly browned, 2 to 3 minutes. Remove the chorizo from the oil with a slotted spoon and set it aside. Add the onion to the pan and cook for 5 minutes, until it begins to soften. Add the bell peppers, garlic, cumin, and dried and fresh oregano and continue to cook the sofrito over medium-low heat, stirring occasionally, until the peppers are tender, 6 to 8 minutes. Place the sofrito, brown sugar, vinegar, and 1 can of the beans in a blender or food processor and puree. Return the puree to the saucepan and stir in the remaining can of beans, the broth, and the chorizo. Season with salt. If the soup seems too thick, add a little more broth. Simmer gently for 8 to 10 minutes to blend the flavors. Ladle the soup into bowls. Pass the garnishes separately.

SERVES 4 TO 6.

⅓ cup olive oil

1 cup chopped chorizo or bacon (optional)

1½ cups chopped red onion (1 medium)

1 red bell pepper, seeded and chopped

1 green bell pepper, seeded and chopped

1 tablespoon minced garlic (2 to 4 cloves)

1 teaspoon ground cumin

1 teaspoon dried oregano leaves

1 tablespoon chopped fresh oregano leaves

1 tablespoon brown sugar

2 tablespoons wine vinegar

2 (15-ounce) cans black beans with their liquid

1 cup *Caldo de Res* (Beef Broth; page 46)

Salt to taste

Extra-virgin olive oil, finely chopped red onion, chopped fresh cilantro or parsley

# Puré de Calabaza La Esperanza
## Creamy Pumpkin Soup

3 tablespoons olive oil

1½ cups chopped onion (1 medium)

2 teaspoons minced garlic (2 cloves)

½ teaspoon ground cinnamon

¼ teaspoon freshly grated nutmeg

2 pounds calabaza, pie pumpkin, or
   butternut squash, peeled, seeded,
   and diced

4 cups chicken broth

1 cup light cream or half-and-half
   (optional)

Salt to taste

Freshly ground black pepper to taste
   (optional)

4 to 6 Cuban Bread Croutons (recipe
   follows)

1 tablespoon minced fresh parsley

Located in a charming, eclectically decorated bungalow with a tiny, lush garden terrace, La Esperanza is one of Havana's most stylish *paladares*. In both its menu and décor, this restaurant reflects a Cuban creativity that shines through in spite of economic hardship and food shortages. Hubert, who handles the front of the house, and Manolo, the chef, produce interesting and flavorful dishes like this squash soup, using the best of what is available at the market that day. If there is cream in the larder, the soup will be richer, and if not, it will be lighter, but in either case what comes out of the La Esperanza's kitchen will be good.

In a large, heavy saucepan, heat the oil over medium-low heat. Add the onion, garlic, cinnamon, and nutmeg and cook slowly until the onion is translucent, 4 to 5 minutes. Add the calabaza and broth. Bring to a boil over medium-high heat. Cover, reduce the heat to low, and simmer until the calabaza is very tender, about 40 minutes.

In a blender or food processor with a steel knife blade, working in two or three batches, puree the calabaza mixture until smooth. Return the puree to the saucepan and stir in the cream. Season with salt and pepper and heat the soup gently, stirring often, until hot.

Ladle the soup into 4 to 6 individual soup bowls, top each serving with a crouton, and sprinkle with parsley.

SERVES 4 TO 6.

## Cuban Bread Croutons

Olive oil for frying

4 to 6 (⅓- to ½-inch-thick) slices
   day-old Cuban or French bread

In a heavy skillet, heat about ½ inch of oil. When the oil is hot enough that a small cube of bread sizzles when dropped in the oil, add 2 or 3 of the bread slices at a time and fry, turning once, until golden brown, 1 to 2 minutes. Remove the croutons with a slotted spatula and drain well on paper towels.

# Sopa de Maíz
## Creole Corn Soup

6 cups fresh or frozen corn kernels

4 cups chicken broth

²/₃ cup heavy cream

3 tablespoons butter

1½ cups diced calabaza or butternut squash

1 cup diced green bell pepper (1 small)

½ cup chopped white onion

1 cup peeled, seeded, and diced tomato

1 tablespoon minced garlic (2 to 3 cloves)

1 teaspoon salt, or to taste

¼ to ½ teaspoon freshly grated nutmeg, or to taste

2 tablespoons minced fresh parsley (optional)

**C**orn, which the Taino people called *mahiz*, probably first came to Cuba through trade with the Maya of the Yucatán Peninsula several thousand years ago. Though it was not as important as yuca, their principal staple, the native peoples of Cuba cultivated corn along with beans, pumpkins, sweet potatoes, peanuts, and hot chiles. Since those early days, Cubans have celebrated the harvest of the first sweet, tender young ears with special dishes like this fresh corn chowder.

In a blender or food processor with a steel knife blade, combine 4 cups of the corn and 2 cups of the broth. Pulse on and off until pureed. Press the pureed corn through a sieve or strainer into a 3- to 4-quart soup pot. Discard the solids that remain in the strainer. Whisk in the remaining broth and the cream and set aside.

In a large skillet, melt the butter over medium heat. Add the calabaza, bell pepper, and onion. Sauté for 6 to 8 minutes, until the onion is softened and translucent. Add the tomato and garlic and sauté for 2 minutes.

Add the sautéed vegetables and the remaining 2 cups corn to the broth mixture. Bring the soup to a boil. Reduce the heat to medium-low and simmer, stirring occasionally, until the vegetables are tender and the soup has the consistency of a light chowder, about 20 minutes. Season with salt and nutmeg, sprinkle with the parsley, if desired, and serve.

SERVES 4 TO 6.

# Congrí Oriental
## Red Beans and Rice

The cooking of Oriente, Cuba's easternmost province, is often more highly seasoned than food in other parts of the country. *Congrí* is a term that is widely used in New Orleans and throughout the Caribbean. It is of African origin, and always refers to some combination of rice and beans. In Oriente, *congrí* means red beans and rice. The seasonings used to prepare the dish show the influence of the creole cooking of the Dominican Republic and Haiti.

If using dried beans, rinse and soak them overnight in cold water to cover. The next day, add enough additional water to cover by 3 inches. Bring the soaking water to a boil and add the cinnamon stick and bay leaf. Reduce the heat to low, cover, and cook the beans at a bare simmer until tender, 1½ to 3 hours, depending on the dryness of the beans and the altitude at which you are cooking them. As they are cooking, check them occasionally, stir gently, and add more hot water, if necessary. When tender but still firm, season the beans with salt. Set the beans and their liquid aside. The beans may also be cooked in a pressure cooker. See the Glossary (page 181) for instructions.

If using canned beans, drain them and set the beans and their liquid aside.

In a large Dutch oven over medium-low heat, cook the bacon until crisp. Remove the bacon with a slotted spoon and set aside. Add the chorizo and ham to the pot and cook, stirring often, until lightly browned, about 5 minutes. Remove the meats with a slotted spoon and set them aside with the bacon. Pour off all but about 1 tablespoon of drippings from the pan and add the oil. Add the onion and bell peppers and cook, stirring, over medium-low heat until the onion and peppers have softened, 10 to 15 minutes.

Meanwhile, put the garlic cloves through a press into a small bowl. Add the salt, cumin, oregano, and ground cinnamon, if using. Use a fork to mash the seasonings to a paste and add it to the onion and peppers. Add the rice and sauté over medium heat for 2 minutes, stirring to coat the grains with oil. Add the meats, 4 cups of the bean liquid, 3 to 4 cups of the cooked beans, and the chiles. Bring to a boil over medium-high heat. Reduce the heat to low, cover, and simmer until the rice is tender, about 20 minutes. Sprinkle with parsley and serve as a main course.

SERVES 6 GENEROUSLY.

½ **pound dried small red beans, or 3 to 4 cups canned red beans, drained, liquid reserved**

IF USING DRIED BEANS

1 **cinnamon stick, preferably Mexican canela**
1 **bay leaf**
**Salt to taste**

IF USING DRIED OR CANNED BEANS

1 **cup diced thick-sliced bacon**
2 **cups diced Spanish chorizo, or other spicy sausage**
1½ **cups diced ham steak**
¼ **cup olive oil**
1½ **cups chopped onion (1 large)**
1½ **cups chopped green bell pepper (2 medium)**
3 to 4 **cloves garlic**
2 to 3 **teaspoons salt**
1 **teaspoon ground cumin**
½ **teaspoon dried oregano leaves**
¼ **teaspoon ground cinnamon (optional)**
1 **cup medium-grain or long-grain white rice**
2 to 3 **fresh *ajis cachucha* (mild Cuban chiles), seeded and minced (optional)**
¼ **cup minced fresh parsley or cilantro (optional)**

# Ensalada de Papas y Judias Blancas
## White Bean and Potato Salad

½ pound red potatoes, quartered

1 (15-ounce) can small white beans such
as Great Northern

1 small sweet yellow onion or red onion,
cut into paper-thin slices

1½ tablespoons white wine vinegar

½ teaspoon salt, or to taste

¾ teaspoon ground cumin

1 garlic clove, crushed in a garlic press

Freshly ground black pepper to taste
(optional)

⅓ cup extra-virgin olive oil

¼ cup chopped fresh parsley, preferably
flat-leaf parsley

Watercress or lettuce leaves

This is a great salad to serve with grilled meat or poultry. When refrigerated, it lasts for several days and seems to improve in flavor. You may want to double the recipe, just to have some on hand as leftovers!

Put the potatoes in a saucepan with enough lightly salted water to cover by 2 inches. Bring to a boil over medium-high heat. Reduce the heat to medium-low and boil gently until tender when pierced with the tip of a knife, 20 to 30 minutes. Meanwhile, drain, but do not rinse, the beans and place the onion slices in a bowl with ice water to cover.

In a salad bowl, whisk together the vinegar, salt, cumin, garlic, and pepper. Gradually whisk in the oil.

Drain the potatoes, and when cool enough to handle, peel and cube them. Drain the onion slices. Add the potatoes, beans, onion, and parsley to the salad bowl and toss gently. Chill or serve at room temperature. Serve the salad surrounded by watercress leaves.

SERVES 4 TO 6.

# Ensalada de Aguacate y Piña
## Avocado and Pineapple Salad

If someone offers you Cuban guacamole, they are probably referring to this interesting and refreshing salad. Both pineapples and avocados grow well in Cuba and though at first it may seem like an unusual combination, the textures and flavors of the two fruits are complementary. This is a wonderful salad to serve with roast chicken or pork.

Cut the pineapple in half lengthwise. Remove and discard the tough core and use a paring knife to cut out the inner flesh, leaving the sturdy shell; dice the pineapple flesh. Place the diced pineapple and any juice in a large, nonreactive bowl. Set the two pineapple halves aside to use as containers for the salad.

In a small mixing bowl, whisk together the lime juice, vinegar, sugar, and salt. Gradually whisk in the oil, then stir in the onion.

Peel, pit, and dice the avocados. Add the avocado to the pineapple. Drizzle with the dressing and sprinkle with the cilantro. Toss gently and spoon the salad into the pineapple halves. Arrange the pineapple halves on a platter and serve.

SERVES 4 TO 6.

1 ripe pineapple

2 tablespoons fresh lime juice

2 tablespoons white wine vinegar or
distilled white vinegar

3½ tablespoons sugar

¼ teaspoon salt, or to taste

¼ cup extra-virgin olive oil

¼ cup finely chopped red onion

2 large ripe but not mushy Florida
avocados, or 3 to 4 Hass avocados

1 tablespoon chopped fresh cilantro

# Ensalada de Calabaza
## Cuban Pumpkin Salad

1 pound calabaza, pie pumpkin, or
   butternut squash
1 to 2 garlic cloves, crushed in a garlic
   press
1½ teaspoons sugar
¾ teaspoon ground ginger
½ teaspoon salt
½ teaspoon ground cumin
½ teaspoon mild paprika
¼ teaspoon ground cinnamon
Freshly ground black pepper to taste
   (optional)
2 tablespoons white wine vinegar
½ cup extra-virgin olive oil
1 small sweet yellow onion, peeled and
   thinly sliced into rings
1 to 2 tablespoons minced fresh cilantro
   or parsley
Bibb or Boston lettuce leaves

There are many Cuban recipes for cooked vegetable salads, but I especially like this exotically seasoned pumpkin one, inspired by versions served at Cucharamama in Hoboken, New Jersey, and El Bambu, the vegetarian restaurant at the National Botanical Gardens in Havana. Calabaza (West Indian pumpkin) is a variety of squash widely used in Cuban cooking. In the United States, calabazas are sold at some Latin American grocery stores and may also be ordered (see Sources, page 183). Though the flavors are slightly different, small pie pumpkins, sold in October and November, and butternut squash, available year round, are good substitutes for calabaza.

Remove the seeds from the unpeeled calabaza and cut it into 1½-inch chunks. Place in a large saucepan with enough water to cover by 2 inches. Bring the water to a boil over medium-high heat. Reduce the heat to medium-low and simmer until the calabaza is just tender when pierced with the tip of a sharp knife, about 20 minutes. Drain the calabaza and set aside until cool enough to peel.

Meanwhile, in a medium-size mixing bowl use a fork to mash together the garlic, sugar, ginger, salt, cumin, paprika, cinnamon, and pepper. Whisk in the vinegar, then gradually whisk in the oil.

Peel the pumpkin and add it to the dressing in the bowl. Add the onion and cilantro. Toss the salad gently and serve on the lettuce leaves.

SERVES 4 TO 6.

# Machuquillo y Torrejas de Machuquillo
## Mashed Green Plantains and Green Plantain Pancakes

The plantain is an important ingredient in Cuban cooking. Plantains are eaten at all stages of ripeness. When green (*verde*), as in this recipe, they are treated as a vegetable, boiled and mashed like potatoes to make *machuquillo*. Leftover mashed plantains may be formed into cakes (*torrejas*) and skillet-fried until crisp and golden on the outside, hot and fluffy on the inside.

**2 large green plantains**
**3 to 4 cloves garlic, peeled**
**³/₄ cup *chicharrones* (pork cracklings)**
**Salt to taste**
**Freshly ground black pepper to taste (optional)**

❖❖❖ ❖❖❖ ❖❖❖

Bring 1¹/₂ quarts water to a boil in a large saucepan over high heat. With a sharp knife, trim off about 1 inch at the ends of the plantains and discard. Cut the plantain into 3 or 4 pieces, but don't peel them. Add the plantain to the water, cover, reduce the heat to medium-low, and boil the plantains in their skins for 50 to 60 minutes, until tender. Remove the plantains with a slotted spoon and, when cool enough to handle, peel them.

Meanwhile, in a food processor with a steel knife blade, or with a mortar and pestle, chop or crush the garlic together with the cracklings to make a paste. Scrape the paste into a small bowl and set aside.

Transfer the plantain pieces to the food processor and pulse on and off 3 or 4 times, until they have reached the consistency of lumpy mashed potatoes. (Or place in a large mixing bowl and mash with a potato masher.) Stir in the garlic mixture, then taste and season with salt. Serve as a side dish, with roast pork or chicken.

SERVES 4 TO 6.

## Torrejas de Machuquillo | Green Plantain Pancakes

Mold the *machuquillo* into 8 to 12 patties. Dip the patties in the pork cracklings, pressing the cracklings into both sides. In a large skillet over medium-high heat, heat the oil. When hot, add the patties and cook until golden brown on both sides, 2 to 3 minutes per side. Sprinkle with the parsley and serve as a side dish with meat or poultry.

**1 recipe *Machuquillo* (this page)**
**³/₄ cup pork cracklings, chopped**
**2 to 3 tablespoons olive oil**
**1 tablespoon minced fresh parsley or cilantro**

SERVES 4 TO 6.

# Moros y Cristianos
## Black Beans and Rice

2 or 3 slices thick-sliced bacon, diced

1 cup chopped onion

¾ cup chopped green bell pepper

1 to 3 cloves garlic, minced

1½ teaspoons ground cumin

½ teaspoon salt, or to taste

⅛ teaspoon freshly ground black pepper, or to taste (optional)

⅛ teaspoon ground cinnamon (optional)

1 cup long-grain white rice

2 cups cooked *Frijoles Negros* (Classic Cuban-Style Black Beans; page 47), 2 cups of the bean cooking liquid reserved; or 1 (15-ounce) can black beans, drained, liquid reserved

1 tablespoon olive oil

1 to 2 tablespoons minced fresh cilantro or parsley

This version of "Moors and Christians," an all-time Cuban classic, is adapted from a recipe given to us by Frank, a talented young chef who caters for many of Havana's foreign embassies. Since he is usually cooking for large dinners and receptions, Frank normally cooks his own beans. To season them, he adds a small cheesecloth bag containing a bay leaf, a stick of canela (Mexican cinnamon), and 5 or 6 black peppercorns. If you are cooking beans to use in this recipe, follow the basic directions for *Frijoles Negros* on page 47, but omit the onion, garlic, and green pepper and add Frank's seasonings. We especially like the exotic but subtle flavor that cinnamon gives to his recipe. For a similar effect using canned beans, add ground cinnamon to the seasonings as suggested below.

In a large saucepan over low heat, cook the bacon until crisp. Remove it with a slotted spoon and set it aside. Add the onion, bell pepper, and garlic to the bacon drippings in the pan and cook over medium heat, stirring often, for 2 to 3 minutes, until the onion is softened and translucent. Stir in the cumin, salt, pepper, and cinnamon and cook, stirring, for 1 minute. Add the rice and sauté for 1 minute. Add the reserved bean liquid. (If you are using canned beans, add enough water to the liquid to make 2 cups.) Stir and bring to a boil over medium-high heat. Cover, reduce the heat to low, and cook until the rice is almost tender, about 15 minutes. Gently stir in the beans and oil, cover, and continue to simmer over low heat for 10 to 15 minutes, until the rice and beans are tender. Fluff with a fork. Sprinkle with the bacon and the cilantro and serve.

SERVES 4 TO 6.

# Plátanos Maduros Fritos
## Fried Ripe Plantains

Fried ripe plantains, black beans, and rice are traditional accompaniments for most Cuban entrées. Plantains are ripe when the skin is black and peels off easily. When fried, they are crisp and caramelized on the outside and soft and sweet on the inside. Some cooks like to sprinkle them lightly with lime juice before serving.

**2 large, very ripe (black-skinned) plantains**
**Vegetable oil for frying**
**1 lime, cut into wedges (optional)**

Peel the plantains as you would bananas. Cut them on the diagonal into ½-inch slices. In a deep-fryer or large, heavy-bottomed skillet, heat at least 1 inch of oil to 350° F. Fry the plantain slices, a few at a time, until they are brown and caramelized, 3 to 4 minutes. Remove with a slotted spoon and drain on paper towels. Serve immediately, or keep them warm in a 200° F. oven until serving time. Serve with the lime wedges, if desired.

SERVES 4 TO 6.

# Tostones
## Twice-Fried Plantains

**3 medium-sized green plantains**
**Vegetable oil for frying**
**½ cup warm water, seasoned with**
**    1 teaspoon salt (optional)**
**Salt to taste**

Two of our favorite places in Cuba for eating *tostones* are El Buganvil, on the outskirts of Havana, which serves fried plantain cups as *tostones rellenos*, filled with picadillo, black beans, or crab salad, and Vista Mar, a stylish restaurant located in a 1950s modern house with a great view of Havana Harbor, where the chef tops flattened, partially cooked plantain slices with small, wafer-thin rounds of raw plantain.

*Tostones* should be crisp and golden on the outside and tender on the inside. One of the secrets to making good *tostones* is to simmer the rounds gently in oil the first time, so that they cook until tender in the middle and don't get too hard and brittle to flatten. *Tostones* are flattened, using a wooden gadget called a *tostonera*, or the bottom of a small glass or the palm of your hand. Before the final frying, drain the flattened slices on paper towels. Some cooks dip the slices in warm salted water to season them, and then set them aside. The final frying, done just before serving, should be in hot oil to crisp the outside.

With a sharp knife, make 3 or 4 long cuts from end to end just through the skin of the plantains. Trim off and discard about 1 inch at each end. Peel, then slice the plantains into ¾-inch-thick rounds for flat *tostones* and 1½-inch-thick rounds for *tostones rellenos*.

In a deep-fryer or deep, heavy skillet, heat at least 1½ inches of oil to 340° F. Lower small batches of plantain slices into the oil and fry gently until tender and just beginning to turn golden, 2 to 3 minutes for ¾-inch rounds and 3 to 4 minutes 1½-inch rounds. Remove the rounds and drain them on paper towels. While still warm, flatten them to about half their original thickness. If making *tostones rellenos*, press the flattened but still warm and flexible slices gently into a ¼-cup measure to form cups. Let the cups rest until slightly firm, then carefully remove them from the measuring cup. *Tostones* may be prepared to this stage and refrigerated for up to one day or frozen for several weeks.

If dipping the slices in warm salt water, do so at this stage, and then place them on paper towels to drain. When ready to serve, heat the oil in the deep-fryer or skillet to 375° F. Lower a small batch of *tostones* into the hot oil and fry until crisp and golden, 1 to 2 minutes for flat *tostones* and 2 to 3 minutes for cups. Remove the slices or cups, drain well on paper towels, and sprinkle with salt. Serve immediately if possible, or keep warm in a 200° F. oven until ready to serve.

**MAKES ABOUT 30 *TOSTONES* OR 15 CUPS; SERVES 4 TO 8.**

# Palitos de Yuca Frita
## Fried Yuca Sticks

Our panel of tasters agreed unanimously that fried yuca is even better than french fries! The outside of these delicate golden sticks is extra crisp and the inside is meltingly tender. The traditional way to serve fried yuca is with warm *Mojo Vinegeta* (*Mojo* Dip or Salad Dressing; page 49) for dipping.

½ to ¾ pound boiled yuca, cut into
   sticks like medium-sized french fries
Vegetable oil for deep-frying
Sea salt

In a deep-fryer or deep, heavy skillet, heat at least 2 inches of oil to 375° F. Add the yuca sticks a few at a time and fry until golden on all sides, 4 to 6 minutes. Drain the yuca on paper towels and keep warm in 200° F oven until all have been fried. Sprinkle the sticks with salt and serve immediately.

SERVES 4 TO 6.

# Longostas Enchiladas
## Lobster in Spicy Tomato Sauce

3 pounds (4 or 5) Florida lobster tails

½ cup olive oil

1½ cups chopped white onions

1½ cups chopped bell peppers (red, green, yellow, or a combination)

1 cup tomato sauce

1 cup white wine

2 tablespoons white balsamic vinegar

1 tablespoon minced garlic (2 to 3 cloves)

1 to 2 *ajis cahucha*, seeded and minced; or ⅛ to ¼ teaspoon ground cayenne pepper (optional)

½ teaspoon sugar

Salt and freshly ground black pepper to taste

1 bay leaf

⅓ cup chopped flat-leaf parsley

Lobsters are abundant in Cuban waters, but since the bulk of the catch is exported, they are a delicacy that seldom reaches the table of ordinary Cubans. Even in expensive government tourist restaurants and *paladares* (private restaurants), where the prices are in convertible pesos, lobster is not officially on the menu, though it is often offered verbally as a special. One of the most traditional Cuban recipes for both lobster and shrimp is this simple preparation with a sofrito of onion and bell pepper in a spicy, but not incendiary, tomato sauce. We have been fortunate to taste excellent *langostas enchiladas* both in Havana and Miami. Serve the lobster with hot fluffy white or yellow rice.

With a sharp chef's knife, cut through the shell and flesh of the lobster tails at each joint, dividing them into sections. Use a toothpick or small skewer to push out the reddish vein that runs down the back of each segment of the tail.

In a large, heavy sauté pan or deep skillet over medium heat, heat the oil. Add the lobster sections and sauté until the shells turn red, about 5 minutes. Add the onions and bell peppers and cook, stirring, until the onions turn translucent, 2 to 3 minutes. Stir in the tomato sauce, wine, vinegar, garlic, chile, and sugar. Taste and season with salt and pepper. Add the bay leaf and 2 tablespoons of the parsley; cover and reduce the heat to low. Simmer gently for 20 to 30 minutes, until the lobster meat is firm and opaque. Remove and discard the bay leaf. Sprinkle the lobster with the remaining parsley and serve immediately.

SERVES 4 TO 6.

# Camarones Enchilados
## Creole-Style Shrimp

½ cup olive oil

1½ cups finely diced onion (1 medium)

1½ cups finely diced green bell pepper (1 large)

1 tablespoon minced garlic (about 3 cloves)

½ teaspoon dried oregano leaves

1 bay leaf

1 (10¾-ounce) can tomato puree

½ cup white wine

Salt and freshly ground black pepper to taste

1½ pounds medium-sized shrimp, peeled and deveined

½ cup roasted red peppers, drained and finely diced

Dash of hot pepper sauce (such as Tabasco), or to taste

¼ cup chopped fresh flat-leaf parsley

My friend Juanita Plana was born on a sugar plantation in the Cuban province of Las Villas, but has lived for many years in New York and Miami. Juanita comes from a family of good cooks. *Camarones enchilados* was a speciality of her mother, Emilia Luzarraga. Though it adds a few more minutes to the preparation time, Juanita says that her mother's secret was to cook the sofrito slowly, long enough to let the onion and peppers soften and the flavors blend. This dish is good served with fluffy white rice and fried sweet plantains.

In a large sauté pan over medium heat, heat the oil. Add the onion, bell pepper, garlic, oregano, and bay leaf. Reduce the heat to medium-low and cook the sofrito, stirring occasionally, until the onion and pepper are softened, about 15 minutes. Stir in the tomato puree and wine. Reduce the heat to low, cover, and simmer for 10 minutes, stirring frequently. Taste and season with salt and pepper. Stir in the shrimp and roasted peppers. Cover and simmer gently until the shrimp turn opaque, 6 to 8 minutes. Season with hot sauce, sprinkle with the parsley, and serve.

SERVES 4 TO 6.

# Ajíes Rellenos con Chorizo, Arroz, y Tomate
## Stuffed Peppers with Sausage, Rice, and Tomato

Stuffed peppers is a favorite home-style Cuban dish. Since rice is a staple in Cuba, cooked rice is a popular base for stuffings. The rest of the recipe, however, usually depends upon the creativity of the cook and what is in the pantry or fridge. The peppers may be served with a salad as a light main course, or as a side dish with roasted meat or poultry.

Preheat the oven to 350° F. In a large saucepan, combine 2 cups water, the rice, salt, and bay leaf. Bring to a boil over high heat. Cook, uncovered, until most of the water has been absorbed and craters form on top of the rice, 10 to 15 minutes. Stir the rice with a fork, cover the pan and reduce the heat to low. Cook for an additional 8 to 10 minutes, until the rice is fluffy. Remove and discard the bay leaf and set the rice aside.

In a skillet over medium heat, sauté the chorizo in the oil for 1 to 2 minutes, until just beginning to brown. With a slotted spoon, transfer the chorizo to the rice, then stir in 1 tablespoon of the drippings from the skillet. Add the eggs and 1½ cups of the *Salsa Española*. Stir the mixture gently until well combined. Set aside.

Cut the tops off the bell peppers and remove the seeds and ribs. Place the peppers in a shallow baking dish and fill them with the rice mixture. Pour the remaining *Salsa Española* around the peppers. Cover the pan tightly with aluminum foil and bake on the middle rack of the oven until the peppers are tender but still hold their shape, 60 to 70 minutes. Baste the peppers 2 or 3 times with the pan sauce as they bake. Serve the peppers and sauce directly from the baking dish.

SERVES 4 TO 6.

1 cup long-grain white rice

1 teaspoon salt

1 small bay leaf

¼ pound Spanish chorizo, diced (about 1 cup)

1 tablespoon olive oil

2 large eggs, beaten

1 recipe *Salsa Española* (Spanish Sauce; page 50)

4 medium or 6 small green, yellow, or red bell peppers

# Arroz con Pollo a la Chorrera
## Chicken with Rice Chorrera-Style

3 pounds bone-in chicken breasts,
   thighs, and drumsticks

4 to 6 cloves garlic, peeled

1 teaspoon salt, or to taste

1 teaspoon dried oregano leaves,
   crumbled

½ teaspoon ground cumin

¼ teaspoon freshly ground black pepper
   (optional)

½ cup fresh bitter orange juice, or
   ¼ cup regular orange juice and ¼ cup
   fresh lime juice

¼ cup olive oil

1 cup chopped onion

1 cup chopped green bell pepper

1 cup seeded, diced tomatoes

4 tablespoons tomato paste

¾ teaspoon *bijol* (annatto seed
   seasoning)

2⅔ cups chicken broth

1 bay leaf

1½ cups Valencia or Arborio rice

1 to 1½ cups beer

1 cup fresh or frozen baby peas

1 red or orange bell pepper, roasted,
   peeled, seeded, and cut into strips

2 tablespoons minced fresh parsley,
   preferably flat-leaf parsley

The origin of the phrase *a la Chorrera* is debated by food scholars. Some believe that the name of this Cuban version of *arroz con pollo* refers to the *chorrera*, a lace collar worn by gentlemen in Spanish colonial times, while others trace the name to the nineteenth-century kitchens of the famous Chorrera del Vedado hotel. Early recipes included dry sherry or wine, but more modern versions call for beer. In Cuba today, it is easier and less expensive to buy chicken thighs and drumsticks than breasts, as dark meat is what is most often imported from the United States and other countries. Wherever it originated and whether you use sherry or beer or dark meat or white meat, this is a tasty and attractive-looking dish!

If the breast halves are large, cut them into two smaller pieces each. Place the chicken pieces in a shallow glass or earthenware baking dish. Using a garlic press and a fork or a mortar and pestle, mash the garlic, salt, oregano, cumin, and black pepper, if using, to a paste. Stir in the bitter orange juice and pour the marinade over the chicken. Cover and marinate the chicken, refrigerated, for 1 to 3 hours, turning the pieces occasionally.

Remove the chicken from the marinade and pat dry with paper towels. Reserve the marinade. In a large, heavy Dutch oven over medium heat, heat the oil. Add the chicken in batches, if necessary. Do not crowd the pan. Brown lightly on all sides, about 10 minutes.

Remove the chicken as it browns, and set aside. To the Dutch oven, add the onion, fresh bell pepper, and tomatoes and sauté until onion is translucent, about 5 minutes. Combine the reserved marinade, tomato paste, *bijol*, and broth and add to the sautéed vegetables. Return the chicken to the pot and add the bay leaf. Cover and simmer over medium to medium-low heat for 40 minutes.

Stir in the rice and continue to simmer, covered, for 15 minutes, or until the rice is almost cooked and the liquid is almost completely absorbed. Stir in the beer and peas and continue to simmer until the rice is tender and the chicken is done, about 10 minutes. Taste and add more salt if necessary, discard the bay leaf, and serve garnished with the roasted pepper and parsley.

SERVES 6 TO 8.

# Boliche (Carne Asada)
## Cuban-Style Pot Roast

Juanita Plana is known in Miami as a caterer of elegant parties and the owner of Chef's Corner, a gourmet store and cooking school in Coral Gables. At home, however, her family often asks for *boliche*, a favorite Cuban comfort food. Juanita's recipe is uncomplicated, tasty, and satisfying. When served with crusty Cuban bread, a tomato and watercress salad, and a creamy, rum-flavored flan, it is the perfect dinner on a wet, chilly Florida evening.

Season the meat with salt and pepper. In a Dutch oven just large enough to hold the roast comfortably, heat the oil over medium heat. Add the roast and brown on all sides, for 15 to 20 minutes. Remove the roast with tongs and set aside.

To the oil in the pot, add the onions, garlic, cumin, oregano, and bay leaves and cook, stirring, over medium-low heat for 10 to 12 minutes, until the onions are soft. Stir in the orange juice, tomato sauce, wine, and enough water so that the liquid will cover the meat halfway. Return the roast to the pan.

Over medium-high heat, bring the liquid in the pot to a simmer. Cover and reduce the heat to low or place the Dutch oven in a preheated 325° F. oven. Simmer the roast gently, turning and basting occasionally, for about 2 hours. Add the potatoes and simmer for an additional 30 to 40 minutes, until the meat and potatoes are tender when pierced with a fork.

Remove the roast and potatoes to a platter and keep warm. Taste the sauce and adjust the seasonings if necessary. If the sauce seems thin, place the pot over medium-high heat and cook, stirring, until the sauce is slightly reduced.

Slice the *boliche* and serve with the potatoes and sauce. If desired, sprinkle with the parsley.

SERVES 4 TO 6.

1 eye of the round beef roast (3 to 3½ pounds)

Salt and freshly black ground pepper to taste

¼ cup olive oil

2 medium-sized yellow onions, thinly sliced

1½ tablespoons minced garlic (4 to 5 cloves)

1 teaspoon ground cumin

1 teaspoon dried oregano leaves

2 bay leaves

1 cup fresh orange juice

1 (8-ounce) can tomato sauce

1 cup *vino seco* (Cuban dry cooking wine) or dry white or red wine

6 small to medium-size red potatoes, peeled and quartered

1 to 2 tablespoons minced fresh flat-leaf parsley (optional)

# Chuletas de Puerco Criollas
## Cuban-Style Pork Chops

8 to 12 thin center-cut pork chops, ½ to
  ¾ inch thick

2 to 4 cloves garlic, or to taste

½ teaspoon dried oregano leaves

½ teaspoon ground cumin

½ cup fresh bitter orange juice, or
  ¼ cup regular orange juice and ¼ cup
  fresh lime juice

½ cup dry sherry or *vino seco* (Cuban
  dry cooking wine)

¼ cup *Aceite de Achiote* (Achiote-
  Flavored Olive Oil; page 44), or
  ¼ cup olive oil and 1 teaspoon *bijol*
  (annatto seed seasoning)

Salt to taste

Freshly ground black pepper to taste
  (optional)

1 large onion, thinly sliced into rings

The first pigs arrived in Cuba when Columbus landed on the island in 1492, and pork has been a favorite meat since those early days. Cuban Americans will tell you that the pork in Cuba tastes different from pork in the United States. That might sound like food nostalgia, but after eating the moist and flavorful pork in Cuba, I have to agree. According to my friend Juanita Plana, who grew up in Cuba, one of the secrets of Cuban pork is that the pigs are fed on *palmiche*, the fruit of a palm tree.

This traditional pork chop recipe is one of my favorites, because it is good, and quick, and easy to prepare. It was a special on the menu the last time Marty and I ate at El Bouganvil, a popular *paladar* (private restaurant) in Havana, and preparing it makes me remember that beautiful balmy evening and the restaurant's lovely garden. There is a little nostalgia attached to most good food memories!

Serve the chops with *Torrejas de Machuquillo* (Green Plantain Pancakes; page 63) or *Plátanos Maduros Fritos* (Fried Ripe Plantains; page 65) and *Moros y Cristianos* (Black Beans and Rice; page 64).

Place the pork chops in a nonreactive baking dish. Crush the garlic in a garlic press, then mix it with the oregano and cumin to form a paste. Rub the paste over the chops. Add the bitter orange juice and sherry. Cover and marinate, refrigerated, for 1 to 4 hours. Remove the chops from the marinade and pat dry with paper towels. Reserve the marinade.

Place the *Aceite de Achiote* in a large skillet over medium-high. When it is sizzling hot, add the chops in small batches and sear until golden brown, 2 to 3 minutes on each side. As they are browned, remove the chops to a dish, sprinkle with salt and pepper, if using, and set aside.

Add the onion to the skillet and sauté over medium heat until translucent, about 5 minutes. Add the reserved marinade and return the chops to the skillet. Reduce the heat to medium-low and cook, turning the chops once or twice, until cooked through, 3 to 5 minutes. Remove the chops to a warm platter and spoon the onions and pan juices over them. Serve.

SERVES 4 TO 6.

# Harina con Carne de Puerco y Chorizo
## Cuban-Style Polenta with Pork and Chorizo Sausage

**FOR THE PORK**

1 pound lean boneless pork shoulder, cut into bite-size pieces

¼ cup fresh bitter orange juice, or 2 tablespoons regular orange juice and 2 tablespoons fresh lime juice

2 to 3 cloves garlic, crushed in a garlic press or finely minced

½ teaspoon ground cumin

Salt to taste

3 to 4 tablespoons olive oil

½ pound Spanish chorizo, diced

1½ cups chopped onion (1 large)

1 cup chopped green bell pepper (1 medium)

1 (14.5-ounce) can diced tomatoes

½ cup *vino seco* (Cuban dry cooking wine) or dry sherry

1 to 3 *ajis cachucha* (mild Cuban chiles), seeded and minced (optional)

**FOR THE HARINA**

1 cup *harina fina* (finely ground yellow cornmeal; see Sources) or stone-ground yellow cornmeal

2 tablespoons olive oil

2 teaspoons salt, or to taste

2 tablespoons minced fresh flat-leaf parsley or cilantro

When Cubans refer to *harina* ("flour" in Spanish), unless they elaborate, they are referring to finely ground cornmeal. A popular dish in Cuba is *harina* cooked with water, oil, and salt until thick and fluffy and combined with pork, chorizo, chicken, or shellfish that has been cooked in a well-seasoned tomato sauce. It is a great comfort food and makes a satisfying main course when served with crusty bread and a salad.

You will often find this dish referred to as *tamal en cazuela*, "tamale in a pot." According to cooking purists like my friend Carmen, however, classic *tamal en cazuela*, like Cuban tamales, should be made with pureed fresh corn. See the recipe for *Tamal en Cazuela Clásico* on page 80.

Make the pork: Place the pork in a glass bowl. Add the bitter orange juice, garlic, cumin, and salt. Cover and marinate, refrigerated, for 2 to 3 hours. Remove the pork from the marinade and pat dry with paper towels. Reserve the marinade.

Place 3 tablespoons of the oil in a large sauté pan or heavy skillet over medium-high heat. When the oil begins to smell fragrant, add the pork, working in two or three batches, making sure that the pieces don't touch. Reduce the heat to medium-low and cook, turning as needed, until the pieces are golden brown on all sides, about 10 minutes. Remove the pork with a slotted spoon as it is browned, and set aside. Add the chorizo to the pan and cook until very lightly browned, about 5 minutes. Add the onion and bell pepper and additional oil, if needed. Cook, stirring, until the onion is translucent and the pepper has softened, 10 to 12 minutes. Stir in the tomatoes, wine, reserved marinade, and chiles. Return the pork to the pan. Cover and simmer gently for 30 minutes, stirring occasionally.

Meanwhile, make the *harina*: In a large, heavy-bottomed saucepan, combine the *harina*, 5 cups cold water, the oil, and salt. Bring to a simmer over medium-high heat, stirring often. Reduce the heat to medium and continue to cook, stirring. When the mixture begins to thicken and bubble, after 10 to 12 minutes, stir in 1 more cup cold water. Cover and reduce the heat to medium-low to low. Cook, stirring often, until the cornmeal thickens to a fluffy but spoonable consistency, about 15 minutes.

To serve, either add the pork mixture to the *harina* and continue to cook, stirring, until heated through and well combined, or reheat the pork mixture separately and spoon it over the *harina* when serving. In either case, serve in wide shallow soup bowls and sprinkle with the parsley.

SERVES 4 TO 6.

# Ropa Vieja de Raquel
## Raquel's Shredded Beef

A favorite lunch destination outside Havana is La Casa de Campesino, a restaurant located on a small farm on what was once a French-owned coffee plantation. Seated under a shady thatched veranda, we watched the antics of the farm cats, dogs, chickens, and a gloriously colorful peacock while enjoying classic country dishes like *masitas de puerco*, velvety black beans, fluffy white rice, *ropa vieja*, and a salad of perfectly ripe tomatoes and crisp cucumbers, thinly sliced and simply dressed with olive oil and vinegar. I especially liked the *ropa vieja*, and the chef, Raquel, generously shared her recipe with me. The recipe for *Caldo de Res* (Beef Broth; page 46) produces the flavorful flank steak used here. Serve this over *Arroz Blanco* (White Rice; page 45).

Place the oil in a large skillet over medium heat. Add the onion and garlic and cook, stirring occasionally, until the onion is translucent, 4 to 5 minutes. Add the bell pepper and sauté for 1 to 2 minutes. Stir in the ketchup, tomato sauce, and wine. Add the shredded flank steak and simmer over medium-low heat, stirring gently, for about 10 minutes to blend the flavors. Season with salt. Sprinkle with the cilantro and serve.

SERVES 4 TO 6.

¼ cup olive oil

½ cup finely chopped onion

1 tablespoon minced garlic (2 to 3 cloves)

1 red bell pepper, seeded and cut into thin strips

¼ cup ketchup

½ cup tomato sauce

½ cup *vino seco* (Cuban dry cooking wine) or white wine

1½ pounds cooked shredded flank steak (see page 46)

Salt to taste

1 to 2 tablespoons chopped fresh cilantro or parsley

# Picadillo Clásico
## Beef Picadillo

1½ tablespoons olive oil

¾ cup diced onion

¾ cup chopped green bell pepper

1 tablespoon minced garlic (2 to 3 cloves)

1½ pounds lean ground beef

⅔ cup tomato sauce

⅓ cup sliced pimiento-stuffed green olives, drained

⅓ cup raisins

1½ tablespoons brine-packed capers, drained

3 tablespoons white wine vinegar or dry sherry

½ teaspoon ground cumin

½ teaspoon dried oregano leaves, crumbled

¼ to ½ teaspoon sugar, or to taste

Salt to taste

Picadillo is a spicy, but not "hot," chopped or ground meat dish that falls somewhere between hash and mincemeat. It is usually made with beef, but there are also versions with pork, lamb, turkey, or fish. Picadillo is tasty and versatile. In Cuba, it is often served as a main course over fluffy rice, with black beans and fried plantains, or used as a filling for empanadas, stuffed potatoes, or shepherd's pie.

In a large skillet over medium heat, heat the oil. Add the onion and bell pepper and sauté until the onion is translucent and softened, about 8 minutes. Add the garlic and cook for 2 minutes more.

Add the beef and sauté until lightly browned, about 5 minutes. Stir in the tomato sauce, olives, raisins, capers, vinegar, cumin, oregano, sugar, and salt. Reduce the heat to low, cover, and simmer for 20 minutes, or until the mixture's consistency is like that of a sloppy Joe. Serve hot or use as a filling.

SERVES 4 TO 6.

# Pollo Frito a la Criolla
## Creole Fried Chicken

For Cubans and tourists alike, El Aljibe is a popular lunch or dinner destination in Havana. The large open-air restaurant has a casual, bustling atmosphere. The specialty of the house is chicken, and the recipe is a closely guarded family secret. One given is that the chicken is first marinated in a traditional *mojo* marinade. The next step in the recipe, however, is hotly debated by culinary detectives. Is the marinated chicken dusted with flour and deep-fried until crisp, or is it roasted in the oven, or is it fried until crisp, then finished in the oven? This is my interpretation of the recipe, in which the chicken comes out crisp on the outside and moist and tender inside. Serve with additional *mojo* sauce, and fluffy white rice and black beans.

If the chicken breast halves are large, cut each into two smaller pieces. Place the chicken in a shallow, nonreactive pan. Crush the garlic in a garlic press into a small mixing bowl. Add the salt and cumin and, using a fork, mash the garlic and seasonings to a paste. Stir in the bitter orange juice, then pour the mixture over the chicken, turning the pieces to coat them thoroughly. Cover and marinate the chicken, refrigerated, for at least 3 hours, turning occasionally.

Remove the chicken from the marinade and pat dry with paper towels. Combine the flour and paprika in a shallow baking pan. Dip the chicken in the seasoned flour, coating thoroughly, then place the pieces on a rack to allow the flour to dry slightly and adhere. In a deep-fryer or deep, heavy skillet, heat at least 2 inches of oil to between 340 and 360° F. Fry the chicken in small batches, turning the pieces frequently with tongs if frying in a skillet, until the chicken is golden brown on all sides and cooked through, 12 to 15 minutes for breasts and 15 to 20 minutes for thighs and drumsticks. Drain the fried chicken on paper towels and serve.

SERVES 4 TO 6.

3 to 3½ pounds bone-in chicken
breasts, thighs, and drumsticks, or
1 whole cut-up chicken
5 to 6 garlic cloves, peeled
1 teaspoon salt
1 teaspoon ground cumin
½ cup fresh bitter orange juice, or
¼ cup regular orange juice and
¼ fresh lime or lemon juice
¾ cup flour
1 teaspoon paprika
Vegetable oil for deep-frying

# Tamal en Cazuela Clásico
## Classic Tamale in a Pot

2 pounds lean pork shoulder, cut into bite-size pieces

3 cloves garlic, crushed in a garlic press

1½ teaspoons salt

½ teaspoon dried oregano leaves

¼ teaspoon ground cumin

¼ cup fresh bitter orange juice, or 2 tablespoons regular orange juice and 2 tablespoons fresh lime juice

8 large ears fresh or frozen corn

¼ cup olive or corn oil

1 cup chopped onion (1 small)

¾ cup chopped green bell pepper (1 small)

2 to 3 *ajis cachuchas* (mild Cuban chiles), seeded and minced (optional)

½ cup tomato sauce

¼ cup *vino seco* (Cuban dry cooking wine)

¼ cup *harina fina* (finely ground yellow cornmeal; optional)

2 tablespoons chopped fresh parsley or cilantro

Carmen and Enrique have a small, word-of-mouth *paladar* (private restaurant) with three tables in the backyard of their house on the road to Camaquey. They have a modest vegetable garden and raise a few pigs and chickens. Carmen cooks good, unpretentious dishes using the fresh produce from her garden. The day that Marty and I stopped by for lunch, she was serving *tamal en cazuela*, one of her specialties, with a salad of tomatoes, cucumbers, and red onion and crusty yuca bread rolls. The fresh sweetness of the corn, the flavor and tenderness of the home-raised pork, and the warm hospitality of our hosts made it a very special meal.

The dish is called *tamal en cazuela* because it is really a thinned-down version of the fresh corn and pork mixture used to make the tamales that are wrapped in corn husks and boiled. When I asked Carmen if, as I had heard, it could also be made with cornmeal, she answered that there was another similar dish made with cornmeal, but that real *tamal en cazuela*, like authentic Cuban tamales, must be made with fresh corn. The corn used to make tamales in Cuba is field corn; it has a higher starch content than the sweet corn sold in the United States. With this in mind, I have taken the liberty of adding a small amount of cornmeal to Carmen's original recipe to thicken the corn puree. If you can get fresh field corn from a local farmer, however, it may be omitted.

Place the pork in a nonreactive container. Mash the garlic, salt, oregano, and cumin together to make a paste, then stir in the bitter orange juice. Pour this marinade over the pork. Cover and refrigerate for 2 to 3 hours.

Husk the corn, and remove and discard the silk. Using a sharp knife, cut off the kernels. Place the cobs in a pan with 3 cups warm water and set aside. In a food processor with steel knife blade, puree the corn. Squeeze the cobs and use the back of a knife to scrape as much of the corn milk as possible into the soaking water. Mix this corn water into the corn puree and press the mixture through a coarse sieve into a bowl. Set aside.

Remove the pork from the marinade with a slotted spoon and pat dry with paper towels. Reserve the marinade. In a Dutch oven over medium-high heat, heat the oil until it is fragrant, then add as many pieces of pork as will fit easily in one layer without touching. Reduce the heat to medium and brown the pork on all sides, 8 to 10 minutes. As it is browned, remove the pork and set it aside. Continue until all the pork has been browned.

To the drippings in the pot, add the onion, bell pepper, and chiles, if using. Cook over medium-low heat, stirring frequently, until the onion and peppers are softened, 10 to 15 minutes. Return the meat to the pan and stir in the tomato sauce, wine, reserved marinade, and corn mixture. Bring to a simmer over medium-high heat, stirring constantly. If using sweet corn instead of field corn, combine the cornmeal with ½ cup cold water and stir it into the pot. Reduce the heat to low, cover, with the lid slightly askew, and simmer gently, stirring frequently, until the corn thickens to a porridgelike consistency, 45 minutes to 1 hour. Taste and adjust the seasonings. Ladle the *tamal* into wide shallow soup bowls. Sprinkle with the parsley and serve.

**SERVES 4 TO 6.**

# Tambor de Maíz con Pollo
## Corn and Chicken Pie

2½ to 3 pounds bone-in chicken breasts
    and thighs

Salt to taste

Freshly ground black pepper to taste
    (optional)

¼ to ½ teaspoon ground cumin to taste

½ lime

¼ to ½ cup olive oil

1½ cups chopped onion (1 large)

¾ cup chopped green bell pepper
    (1 small)

¾ cup chopped red bell pepper (1 small)

2 to 3 teaspoons minced garlic (2 to 3
    cloves)

1 (15-ounce) can diced or crushed
    tomatoes

½ cup dry sherry or *vino seco* (dry
    Cuban cooking wine)

½ cup sliced pimiento-stuffed green
    olives

2 tablespoons brine-packed capers,
    drained

5 cups fresh or frozen corn kernels

1½ cups heavy cream

1 tablespoon sugar

6 egg yolks

¼ cup freshly grated Parmesan cheese

A *tambor* is a Cuban shepherd's pie. *Tambor* is an everyday family kind of dish, and there are many versions with different toppings and fillings. This one, made with fresh, young corn as a topping and tender diced chicken in savory tomato sauce as a filling, is a favorite of mine. Serve it as a main course, accompanied by a crisp cucumber salad and warm, crusty yuca bread rolls.

Rinse the chicken pieces under cold running water and pat dry with paper towels. Season with salt, pepper, cumin, and a squeeze of lime juice. Place 4 tablespoons of the oil in a large, heavy-bottomed Dutch oven or sauté pan over medium heat. When the oil is hot, add the chicken pieces and cook, turning occasionally, until golden brown on all sides, 10 to 12 minutes. Reduce the heat to medium-low, cover and cook gently until the chicken is tender and cooked through, 10 to 20 minutes. Remove the chicken to a platter and set it aside until cool enough to handle.

Add 2 to 3 tablespoons of the remaining oil to the pan. Stir in the onion, bell peppers, and garlic. Cook over low to medium-low heat, stirring often, until the vegetables have softened and the onion is translucent, 10 to 12 minutes. Add the tomatoes and cook, stirring occasionally, for another 15 to 20 minutes. Remove 1 cup of the tomato mixture and set it aside. Stir the sherry, olives, and capers into the remaining tomato mixture. Taste and season with cumin. Cover with the lid slightly askew. Simmer the sauce over low heat until slightly thickened, 10 to 15 minutes. Set aside.

Remove and discard the skin and bones from the chicken. Cut the meat into bite-sized pieces and add it to the tomato sauce. Taste and adjust the seasonings if necessary. Set aside.

Preheat the oven to 350° F. Oil an 8-by-12-by-2½-inch baking dish.

In a food processor with a steel knife blade, or in a blender, puree the corn. In a large, heavy-bottomed saucepan, combine the puree with the cream, sugar, and the reserved 1 cup tomato sauce. Taste and adjust the seasonings. Cook the corn mixture, uncovered, over medium heat, stirring often, until the mixture thickens to the consistency of oatmeal. Remove from the heat, then whisk in the egg yolks one at a time.

Spoon the chicken into the baking dish and cover it with the corn mixture. Bake for 30 minutes. Sprinkle the top with the cheese, then return the *tambor* to the oven and bake until the top is nicely browned, 10 to 15 minutes. Serve the *tambor* directly from the baking dish.

SERVES 6.

# Arroz con Leche
## Cuban Rice Pudding

**S**ometimes the simplest things are best. I have tasted and tested several different versions of Cuban rice pudding. Some recipes are quite complex and include cream, milk, condensed milk, evaporated milk, and long periods of constant stirring and fussing. The best technique for making rice pudding I have found is the straightforward one suggested by chef and award-winning cookbook author Josefa "Jo" Gonzales-Hastings in her cookbook *La Habana Café*. Gonzalez-Hasting was born in Cuba and came to Florida with her parents in 1966. The family opened the Habana Café in Gulfport, Florida, in 1997. The restaurant and its chef have developed a loyal clientele and gained national recognition for serving high-quality, authentic Cuban food.

This pudding recipe is adapted from Jo's. For variety, I sometimes add raisins or pineapple to the pudding to give it a tropical touch.

In a saucepan, combine the milk, rice, sugar, cinnamon stick, and orange and lime zests. Cook, stirring, over medium heat until the milk comes to a slow boil. Cover and reduce the heat to very low. If you have a flame tamer, use it. Simmer the pudding, stirring occasionally, until it has thickened and the rice is very tender, about 1 hour. Stir in the vanilla and raisins or pineapple, if using. Serve the pudding warm or chilled, sprinkled lightly with ground cinnamon.

**SERVES 4 TO 6.**

4½ cups whole milk

¾ cup medium-grain rice (such as Valencia or Arborio)

½ cup sugar

1 cinnamon stick, preferably Mexican canela

1 strip orange zest

1 strip lime zest

⅛ teaspoon salt

1½ teaspoons pure vanilla extract

½ cup raisins, plumped in 2 tablespoons each hot water and rum, then drained; or 1 (8-ounce) can crushed pineapple, well drained (optional)

Ground cinnamon

# Besitos de Merengue
## Meringue Kisses

1 cup sugar

Coarsely grated zest of 1 lime

3 large egg whites at room temperature

Pinch of cream of tartar

Pinch of salt

½ teaspoon pure vanilla extract

Powdered sugar for dusting (optional)

Since classic Cuban desserts like flan and *natillas* are made with egg yolks, there has to be something to do with all of the whites. Meringues are a logical and delightful solution. Eggs are officially rationed in modern Cuba, so meringues are not as common there as they once were, but at Cuban bakeries like the one at the Café Versailles Miami, they are a popular sweet to eat with a *cafecito*.

For a variation, ¼ cup shredded, sweetened coconut and/or ½ cup chopped, lightly toasted walnuts, hazelnuts, or pecans may be folded into the meringue before baking. If adding these more chunky ingredients (which may block a pastry tip), drop rounded teaspoons of meringue onto the baking sheet instead of using a pastry bag.

Preheat the oven to 200° F. Line a large baking sheet with baking parchment or aluminum foil.

Combine the sugar, ⅓ cup water, and the lime zest in a heavy saucepan. Bring to a simmer over medium-high heat, occasionally swirling the pan by the handle, but not stirring. When the liquid turns from cloudy to clear, cover the pan and reduce the heat to low.

Meanwhile, with an electric mixer, beat the egg whites at low speed until they start to become foamy. Add the cream of tartar and salt, and gradually increase the speed and beat until the whites stand in soft peaks. Stir in the vanilla.

Remove the lid from the sugar syrup and boil over medium-high heat until the temperature on a candy thermometer reaches 238° F. and a few drops of syrup drizzled into a bowl of cold water holds a soft but definite shape. Slowly pour the hot syrup through a coarse strainer into the egg whites while beating at medium speed; discard the lime zest. Continue to beat until the meringue stands in stiff peaks and the outside of the mixer bowl is barely warm to the touch, about 10 minutes.

Using a pastry bag and a ½-inch cannelated tip or a teaspoon, pipe or spoon bite-size rounded mounds of meringue, with a little pointed top, about 1 inch apart on the baking parchment. Place the baking sheet on the middle rack of the oven. Keep the oven door slightly ajar and bake the meringues until they can be gently loosened from the parchment with a spatula, about 1 hour. Remove from the oven and let the meringues cool completely on the baking sheet. The finished *besitos* should be white, crisp, and light.

MAKES 24 TO 30 *BESITOS.*

# Boniatillo
## Sweet Potato Pudding

**B**oniato (white sweet potato) is one of the most versatile and traditional Cuban crops. It is eaten as a vegetable and also used to make desserts. The texture of *boniatillo*, a rich, sweet pudding, is a bit like a light sweet potato pie without the crust. *Boniatillo* is also the base of the delectable *Cake de Boniato* (Sweet Potato Cake) on page 90.

❖❖ ❖❖ ❖❖

Peel and cube the *boniatos*. Place them in a large saucepan with enough water to cover by 2 inches. Bring to a boil over high heat. Reduce the heat to medium-low and simmer, uncovered, until tender, about 30 minutes. Drain the *boniatos* and press them through a potato ricer or mash them. Set the puree aside while making the syrup.

In a large, deep skillet, combine the sugar, $2/3$ cup water, the lime zest, and cinnamon stick. Cook, stirring, over medium-low heat until the mixture turns clear and forms a syrup. Remove the lime zest and cinnamon stick. Stir the *boniato* puree into the syrup and cook, stirring, until the mixture is well combined. Remove from the heat, then gradually whisk in the egg yolks and the rum, if using. Return to medium-low heat and cook, stirring constantly, until the mixture reaches a puddinglike consistency. Spoon the pudding into individual dessert bowls. Serve warm or chilled, topped with whipped cream and lightly sprinkled with ground cinnamon.

**SERVES 4 TO 6.**

1 pound *boniatos* (white sweet potatoes)
   or other sweet potatoes
1½ cups sugar
½-inch-wide strip lime zest
1 cinnamon stick
2 large egg yolks, beaten
1 to 2 tablespoons rum (optional)
½ cup lightly sweetened whipped cream
Ground cinnamon

# Brazo Gitano
## Basic Jelly-Roll Cake

1 to 2 tablespoons butter, softened, for the pan

6 large eggs, separated

6 tablespoons sugar

6 rounded tablespoons cake flour

½ teaspoon baking powder

¼ teaspoon salt

1 teaspoon pure vanilla extract

1 to 2 tablespoons powdered sugar

**B**razo gitano ("Gypsy arm") is the Cuban version of a jelly roll. It is a versatile cake. When spread with guava puree, rolled up, and dusted with powdered sugar, it's a comfort food, easy enough to make for a weeknight family dinner. But filled with rich custard, frosted with swirls of glossy meringue, and drizzled with caramel, it's a dessert that shines on special occasions. The most elegant cakes in Miami, including brazos gitano, are made by Lucila Venet Jimenez. At the five bustling locations of her bakery, Sweet Art by Lucila, customers line up to buy cakes and pastries, and brides and their mothers study displays of beautiful wedding cakes. For those who don't live in south Florida, it is also possible to order some of Lucila's specialities through her website (see Sources, page 183). Lucila was kind enough to share with us her basic recipe for brazo gitano, with two different fillings and finishes—one plain and one fancy, and both delicious!

Preheat the oven to 375° F. Butter a 15-by-10-by-1-inch jelly-roll pan and line it with baking parchment. Butter the parchment.

With an electric mixer, beat the egg whites at medium speed until soft peaks form. Gradually add the sugar while increasing the speed to high. Beat until the whites stand in stiff peaks when you lift up the beater. In a separate bowl, beat the egg yolks until fluffy and pale yellow in color. In another bowl, sift together the cake flour, baking powder, and salt. With a rubber spatula, gently fold the egg yolks into the whites, then gradually fold in the flour and vanilla.

Pour the batter into the prepared jelly-roll pan and spread it evenly out to the edges of the pan. Bake on the middle rack of the oven until the top is golden and a toothpick inserted in the center comes out clean, about 15 minutes. Use a sharp knife to trim off the crisp edges of the cake. While the cake is still warm, invert it onto a clean, slightly damp kitchen towel that has been dusted with powdered sugar. Carefully peel off and discard the parchment. Roll up the cake in the towel, starting from the shorter side and rolling away from you. Set aside to cool for 5 minutes before filling the cake according to one of the recipes that follow.

MAKES 1 JELLY-ROLL CAKE.

# Brazo Gitano Acaramelado | Custard-Filled Jelly Roll with Meringue and Caramel

At least 2 hours in advance, make the *natilla* (custard) filling: In a heavy 2-quart saucepan, combine the milk with the cinnamon and lemon zest. Bring the milk just to a simmer over medium-high heat. Remove from the heat and set aside.

With an electric mixer or whisk, beat the egg yolks, sugar, and cornstarch until pale yellow. With a slotted spoon, remove the cinnamon and lemon zest from the milk. Gradually add the hot milk to the eggs, whisking constantly. Return the mixture to the saucepan and cook over medium heat, stirring constantly, until the custard is quite thick, 6 to 8 minutes. It will continue to thicken as it cools, but remember that to be a filling it should be spreadable. Remove from the heat and stir in the vanilla. Pour the *natilla* into a bowl, place a sheet of plastic wrap directly on the surface so a skin won't form on top, and refrigerate until well chilled, about 2 hours.

Make the meringue: Combine the sugar, ⅓ cup water, and the lime zest in a heavy saucepan. Bring to a simmer over medium-high heat, occasionally swirling the pan by the handle, but not stirring. When the liquid turns from cloudy to clear, cover the pan and reduce the heat to low.

Meanwhile, with an electric mixer, beat the egg whites at low speed until they start to become foamy. Add the cream of tartar and salt, and gradually increase the speed and beat until the whites stand in soft peaks. Stir in the vanilla.

Remove the lid from the sugar syrup and boil over medium-high heat until the temperature on a candy thermometer reaches 238° F. and a few drops of syrup drizzled into a bowl of cold water holds a soft but definite shape. Slowly pour the hot syrup through a coarse strainer into the egg whites while beating at medium speed; discard the lime zest. Continue to beat until the meringue stands in stiff peaks and the outside of the mixer bowl is barely warm to the touch, about 10 minutes.

Fill the cake: Gently unroll the cooled cake. Evenly spread the *natilla* over the cake, leaving a 1-inch border around the edges uncovered. Carefully roll up the cake, using the towel to help you, and place it seam side down on a work surface. If necessary, use a sharp

*(continued)*

FOR THE *NATILLA* (CUSTARD) FILLING

**2 cups whole milk**

**1 cinnamon stick, preferably Mexican canela**

**1 (¼-inch-wide) strip lemon zest**

**3 large egg yolks**

**½ cup sugar**

**2 tablespoons cornstarch**

**½ teaspoon pure vanilla extract**

FOR THE MERINGUE

**1 cup sugar**

**Coarsely grated zest of 1 lime**

**3 large egg whites at room temperature**

**Pinch of cream of tartar**

**Pinch of salt**

**½ teaspoon pure vanilla extract**

FOR THE CAKE

**1 *Brazo Gitano* (Basic Jelly-Roll Cake; opposite)**

FOR THE CARAMEL

**½ cup sugar**

knife to trim off about ½ inch at each end of the roll to neaten the edges. Carefully transfer the jelly roll to a serving platter.

With a spatula, frost the cake with swirls of meringue, covering the sides and top. If desired, use a pastry bag to add decorative touches. Set aside in a cool, dry place until ready to serve. (The cake can be made ahead up to this point and frozen until firm, then carefully tented with aluminum foil to protect the meringue. The cake will stay fresh in the freezer for up to 2 weeks. Remove it from the freezer and allow it to sit at room temperature for at least 1 hour before serving.)

Make the caramel: Place the sugar and 2 tablespoons water in a saucepan over medium heat. Swirl the pan by the handle until the sugar melts and turns a light amber color. Remove from the heat and use a spoon to drizzle the hot caramel in decorative lines over the meringue. Slice the cake and serve.

SERVES 6 TO 8.

## Brazo Gitano de Guayaba | Guava Jelly Roll

**17.5 ounces guava paste**

**1 to 2 tablespoons fresh orange juice or lemon juice**

**1 tablespoons rum (optional)**

**1 teaspoon finely grated orange or lemon zest (optional)**

**1 *Brazo Gitano* (Basic Jelly-Roll Cake; page 86)**

**2 to 3 tablespoons powdered sugar**

**Lightly sweetened whipped cream (optional)**

Place the guava paste, orange juice, rum, and orange zest in a food processor with the plastic knife blade and pulse until pureed and spreadable.

Gently unroll the cooled cake. Evenly spread the guava mixture over the cake, leaving a 1-inch border around the edges uncovered. Carefully roll up the cake, using the towel to help you, and place it seam side down on a work surface. If necessary, use a sharp knife to trim off about ½ inch at each end of the roll to neaten the edges. Carefully transfer the jelly roll to a serving platter. Sprinkle lightly with the powdered sugar. Slice the cake and serve, dolloped with the whipped cream, if desired.

SERVES 6 TO 8.

# Cake de Boniato
## Sweet Potato Cake

½ cup (1 stick) unsalted butter, melted, plus 1 tablespoon softened butter for the dish

1 recipe *Boniatillo* (Sweet Potato Pudding; page 85)

1 teaspoon pure vanilla extract

2 large eggs, separated

1 cup cake flour

2 teaspoons baking powder

Pinch of salt

Powdered sugar for dusting

Unlike other Spanish-speaking countries in Latin America, a cake in Cuba is a *cake* (pronounced "ka-kay") not a *pastel* or *torta*. In the 1950s, among the gifts every young bride received was a copy of *Cocina al Minuto* (the Cuban equivalent of *The Joy of Cooking*) written by Nitza Villapol and Martha Martinez. During that era, cooking trends from the United States, including cake making, were fashionable in Cuba, and the table of contents of *Cocina al Minuto* lists more than twenty cake recipes.

The cake recipe that follows was probably developed in the 1950s. It combines *boniatillo*, a classic Cuban sweet potato pudding, with the makings of an American-style cake. The result is unusual and absolutely delicious, a cake with fine light crumb and delicate hint of sweet potato.

Preheat the oven to 350° F. Generously butter a 2-quart soufflé dish.

In a mixing bowl, combine the *Boniatillo*, melted butter, and vanilla. Stir in the egg yolks. In a separate bowl, sift together the cake flour, baking powder, and salt. Gradually stir the dry ingredients into the *Boniatillo* mixture. In a separate bowl, beat the egg whites until they stand in firm peaks. Gently but thoroughly fold the *Boniatillo* mixture into the beaten whites. Pour the batter into the prepared soufflé dish. Bake on the middle rack of the oven until the cake is golden on top and a toothpick inserted in the center of the cake comes out clean, about 45 minutes.

Let the cake cool in the dish for 10 minutes, then carefully turn it out onto a rack and let it cool completely. Dust the top of the cooled cake with powdered sugar and serve.

SERVES 6 TO 8.

# Dulce de Fruta Bomba
## Papaya Compote

Eduardo is a talented young chef. When speaking with him about food you can feel his passion for cooking and his pride in the culinary traditions of Cuba. He and his wife, Alicia, and young daughter Ellie live in a modern apartment building in Havana. Marty and I met Alicia at the restaurant where she works, and she generously invited us to join her family and some friends for dinner at their home. The dinner began with a first course of *ajiaco* (beef and vegetable stew), followed by *masitas de puerco* (fried chunks of pork), fluffy white rice, creamy black beans, and boiled yuca with *mojo* sauce. After a refreshing tomato and cucumber salad drizzled with lime juice and olive oil, Eduardo served an exotic compote made with green papaya cooked slowly in a sugar syrup flavored with ginger, cinnamon, and citrus. I asked him how to make it and he was kind enough to share the recipe with us.

Serve the cold compote accompanied by slivers of cream cheese or a scoop of *Helado de Queso Crema* (Cream Cheese Ice Cream; page 157).

In a large, heavy-bottomed saucepan, combine 1½ cups water and the sugar. Place the pan over medium heat and cook, stirring, until the sugar is dissolved and the syrup turns clear, 5 to 6 minutes. Add the cinnamon stick, ginger, if using, and orange and lemon slices and reduce the heat to low. Do not stir, but swirl the pan occasionally by the handle, while preparing the papaya.

Cut the papaya in half lengthwise. Scoop out and discard the seeds. Peel and cut the fruit into 1½- to 2-inch chunks. Toss it with the lime juice and add it to the syrup. Cook over low heat, uncovered, stirring gently from time to time, until a chunk of papaya is tender when pierced with the point of a knife but still holds its shape, 15 to 30 minutes, depending on the ripeness of the fruit. Remove from the heat and let the fruit cool in the syrup. Refrigerate until ready to serve. Serve the papaya in small dessert bowls.

SERVES 4 TO 6.

2 cups sugar

1 cinnamon stick, preferably Mexican canela

1 (½-inch) slice fresh ginger (optional)

1 slice orange

1 slice lime or lemon

1 green (unripe) Caribbean (Mexican) papaya (1 to 1½ pounds)

2 tablespoons fresh lime or lemon juice

# Flan de Leche Clásico
## Classic Flan

**FOR THE CARAMEL**

½ cup sugar

**FOR THE CUSTARD**

4 large egg yolks

3 large whole eggs

¾ cup sugar

Pinch of salt

2 cups half-and-half or whole milk

1 cinnamon stick, preferably Mexican
   canela

1 (1-inch) strip lime zest

1 vanilla bean, or 1 teaspoon pure vanilla
   extract

1 tablespoon light rum (optional)

This is a rich old-fashioned flan. My friend Marta recalls that, when she was a child in the 1950s, the fresh milk delivered to her family's home, in Piñar del Rio, had heavy cream floating on the top. Her grandmother's cook Josefa, who was known for her desserts, always mixed the cream into the milk when making flan.

The only challenging step in making a flan is caramelizing the mold. Experienced Cuban cooks often melt the sugar directly over the burner in the metal mold. I prefer to make caramel in a saucepan and then pour it into the mold. Even with good oven mitts, the mold gets very hot to handle. It is easier to hold a saucepan by the handle and stir the sugar until it melts and turns the desired amber color. If the caramel hardens when you are using a metal mold, place it over low heat to melt the caramel, then tilt it to evenly coat the bottom and sides. If using a porcelain mold, place it in a microwave at low power for 20 to 30 seconds.

Make the caramel: Place the sugar in a medium-sized heavy bottomed saucepan over medium heat. Cook, stirring constantly, until the sugar melts and turns a light amber color, 10 to 15 minutes.

Make the custard: Preheat the oven to 350° F.

In a large mixing bowl, beat the egg yolks, whole eggs, sugar, and salt until the mixture is fluffy and pale yellow.

Pour the half-and-half into a heavy, medium-sized saucepan. Add the cinnamon stick, lime zest, and vanilla bean (if using vanilla extract, add it later). Bring the half-and-half just to a simmer. Remove from the heat and let the half-and-half steep for a few minutes. Remove and discard the cinnamon stick and lime zest. Slit the vanilla bean down one side with a sharp knife and scrape the pulp of the bean into the half-and-half (or add the vanilla extract, if using). Stir in the rum, if using.

Gradually beat the hot half-and-half mixture into the egg mixture. Pour the custard through a strainer into the mold and place the mold in a larger baking pan. Place the pan on the middle rack of the oven and pour in enough boiling water to come halfway up the sides of the mold.

Lower the oven temperature to 325° F. and bake for 40 to 50 minutes, until a skewer or knife inserted in the center of the flan comes out clean. Carefully lift the flan out of the water bath and place it on a baking rack to cool. When cool, refrigerated the flan until chilled, at least 1 hour. When cold, run a thin-bladed knife around the edges of the flan. Place a serving plate face down on top of the mold. Gripping the mold and plate together with both hands, invert the flan onto the plate. Slice and serve with the caramel from the mold.

**SERVES 4 TO 6.**

# Pan Dulce de Calabaza
## Sweet Pumpkin Bread

1½ cups all-purpose flour

1 teaspoon baking powder

1 teaspoon ground cinnamon

1 teaspoon freshly grated nutmeg

½ teaspoon salt

¼ teaspoon ground allspice

1 cup cooked and pureed fresh calabaza
   or canned pumpkin puree

¾ cup sugar

½ cup (1 stick) unsalted butter, melted

2 large eggs, beaten

½ cup golden raisins (optional)

Calabaza, West Indian pumpkin, is used to make both sweet and savory dishes in Cuba. It is a large squash with a hard, tannish-gold or green skin and vivid orange-colored flesh. It may weigh as much as twenty pounds, so you often see shoppers at Cuban farmer's markets buying calabaza by the pound from a vendor who cuts off chunks with machete.

Though it is possible to find fresh calabazas at some Latin American grocery stores in the United States, and they also may be ordered (see Sources, page 183), good substitutes are fresh pie pumpkin or butternut squash or canned pumpkin. To prepare calabaza puree: Carefully cut the calabaza in half with a large, heavy chef's knife. Remove the seeds and cut the flesh into chunks. Boil or steam the chunks until tender when pierced with the tip of a knife. When cool enough to handle, remove the peel with sharp paring knife, then puree the flesh.

Sweet quick bread recipes like this one reflect the strong influence of cooking trends that originated in the United States on the Cuban cooking of the 1940s and '50s. This is a great breakfast, tea, or dessert bread.

Preheat the oven to 350° F. Butter a 9-by-5-inch loaf pan and line the bottom with baking parchment or waxed paper.

In a medium bowl, sift together the flour, baking powder, cinnamon, nutmeg, salt, and allspice.

Place the calabaza puree, sugar, butter, and eggs in a large mixing bowl and thoroughly combine with an electric mixer. With the mixer at low speed, gradually add the flour mixture. Fold in the raisins. Spoon the batter into the prepared loaf pan. Bake on the middle rack of the oven until the loaf has risen and a toothpick inserted in the center comes out clean, 50 to 60 minutes. Let the loaf cool in the pan on a wire rack for 10 minutes, then turn it out onto the rack, peel off the paper, and let it cool completely before serving.

MAKES 1 (9-BY-5-BY-3-INCH) LOAF.

# Pan Cubano
## Cuban Bread

When she was growing up in Las Villas, Juanita Plana remembers that the top of each warm, fragrant loaf from the local *panaderia* was decorated with a single palm leaf. There are two traditional kinds of bread in Cuba, *pan de agua* (water bread), made with just yeast, flour, salt, and water, and *pan de manteca* (lard bread), which has melted lard added for moisture. Both are tender and fluffy on the inside and crusty on the outside. *Pan de agua* is the Cuban bread most often sold in both Havana and Miami, but I've chosen to include a recipe for *pan de manteca* here because it stays fresh a little longer. To make *pan de agua*, simply omit the lard or butter.

1 (¼-ounce) package active dry yeast
1 tablespoon sugar
1 tablespoon salt
5 to 6 cups sifted all-purpose flour
4 tablespoons melted lard or butter
2 tablespoons cornmeal
6 to 8 bay leaves (optional)

In a large mixing bowl, dissolve the yeast and sugar in 2 cups lukewarm water, stirring well. Set aside in a warm place until the yeast bubbles actively, 8 to 10 minutes. Combine the salt with 3 cups of the flour. Add this flour mixture to the yeast mixture, 1 cup at a time, beating it in with a wooden spoon or using the dough hook of an electric mixer at low speed. After each cup of flour, drizzle in about 1 tablespoon of lard. Once you have added the first 3 cups, use your hands to gradually knead in the remaining flour until the dough is smooth and velvety. Gather the dough into a ball and place it in a clean greased mixing bowl. Grease the top of the dough with the remaining lard. Cover with a dry, clean kitchen towel and place in a warm (80 to 90° F.), draft-free area to rise until doubled in bulk, about 1 hour.

Turn the dough out onto a lightly floured board and divide it in half. Shape each piece of the dough by stretching and rolling it into a long sausage shape about 1 foot long and 2 inches in diameter.

Arrange the loaves 2 to 3 inches apart on a large baking sheet sprinkled with the cornmeal. Cover lightly with the towel and let the loaves rise for 5 to 7 minutes.

Using a sharp knife, slash each loaf in 3 or 4 places and, if desired, place a bay leaf in each slit to decorate the loaf. Brush the loaves with water. Place a pan of boiling water in the bottom of the oven. Immediately place the baking sheet on the middle rack of the cold oven and set the oven temperature 400° F. Bake the loaves until they are crusty and sound hollow when tapped gently on top, 35 to 45 minutes. Remove the loaves to a rack to cool.

**MAKES 2 LOAVES.**

# THREE | Comidas Ambulantes ▣ Street Food

# Comidas Ambulantes | Street Food

My first meal in Cuba was street food. Driving from Jose Marti International Airport into Havana, Marty and I are intrigued by carts and kiosks along the road selling all kinds of food, from snow cones to empanadas (fried pies). It's lunchtime and people have begun to line up in front their favorite stands. Through the open car windows we inhale an exotic potpourri of fried dough, grilling meat, and flowering trees mixed with the fumes of leaded gas. An artistically decorated trailer with a sign advertising "Pizza" catches our eye. Is Cuban pizza really different? We ask the driver to pull over so we can take a picture, and give it a try. It's good, and somehow it is different, the same basic ingredients as other pizza, but here it tastes more . . . more Cuban.

Street food is popular in Cuba, part of a longstanding tradition of stopping during the day for a *cafecito* (a tiny cup of strong coffee) and a *bocadito* (a snack). It's a chance to get together with friends for a few minutes and just take a break.

Opening a food stand is an opportunity for Cuban entrepreneurs to have their own business, and a way for customers who can't afford to go to restaurants to enjoy eating out and socializing. There is street food for most any mood and budget. For breakfast on the run, stop at the corner coffee cart for a *cortadito* (coffee with hot milk) and a *rosquilla* (doughnut). Feeling hungry but poor? Try a *croqueta* (croquette) or *fritura* (fritter)—they are tasty, inexpensive, and filling. If you want to splurge, order a pizza or *frita* (Cuban hamburger), or a *sandwich Cubano*, half a loaf of Cuban bread, split and spread with mustard and mayo and filled with ham, cheese, roast pork, and pickles and toasted in a giant sandwich press.

We enjoyed doing the research for this chapter. Street food is fun to begin with, but even more memorable is the experience of meeting everyday Cubans. Wherever we went, people at the food stands, both cooks and customers, were hospitable, and glad to share recipes with us. We have included some of our favorites and hope that when you taste them you'll be transported at least for a moment to this fascinating island.

# Sandwich Cubano La Ideal
## La Ideal's Cuban Sandwich

2 loaves *Pan Cubano* (Cuban Bread; page 95) or French bread

2 to 3 tablespoons yellow mustard

¼ cup mayonnaise

2 or 3 dill pickles, cut into long, thin slices

⅓ to ½ pound thinly sliced Swiss cheese

⅓ to ½ pound thinly sliced ham

⅓ to ½ pound shredded or thinly sliced *Puerco Asado* (Roast Pork Loin; page 53)

3 to 4 tablespoons melted butter

Located in what was once an old grocery store, La Ideal is a favorite neighborhood hangout for members of Tampa's Cuban-American community. The scene is animated and relaxed. Regulars chat from table to table, but the feeling is inclusive, with visitors made to feel like members of the family.

A dynamic force behind the atmosphere at La Ideal is Majito, Mario Aguila Jr. Majito's dad, Mario Sr., moved his family to the United States from Cuba in 1966. After ten years in New York, the family settled in Tampa and opened La Ideal. In 2005 Mario Sr. sold La Ideal to Luis and Juanita Tejada. The ownership has changed, but Majito has stayed on at the front of the house, and with Juanita in charge in the kitchen, the food is still great. Cuban sandwiches, toasted in a large sandwich press, are a specialty of the house.

Pork is the most popular meat in Cuba, and if they have the room, many Cuban families keep a pig or two. Pigs are easy to care for, and if there is a special occasion like a daughter's fifteenth birthday or a wedding, the pig may either be slaughtered for the feast or sold to pay for the celebration.

◈◈ ◈◈ ◈◈

Trim the ends off the bread loaves, then cut the loaves into 8-inch sections. Split the sections in half lengthwise. Spread mustard on the cut side of each bottom half and mayonnaise on each top half. Layer pickle slices on top of the mustard, then add layers of cheese, ham, and *Puerco Asado*. Place the other half of the bread on top, mayonnaise side down. Preheat a sandwich or panini press, or, if you don't have one, preheat the oven to 350° F. Brush the tops of the sandwiches with butter. Put the sandwiches in the press (or arrange them on a nonstick baking sheet and place another baking sheet on top; weight down the baking sheet with a heavy iron skillet or a brick wrapped in aluminum foil). Press or bake the sandwiches until they are crisp and golden brown and the cheese has melted, 6 to 8 minutes. Cut the sandwiches in half on the bias and serve.

**MAKES 4 LARGE SANDWICHES; SERVES 4 TO 8.**

# Pan con Bistec
## Steak Sandwich

4 thin beef breakfast steaks

2 teaspoons minced garlic (1 to 2 cloves)

¼ cup fresh lime juice

Salt and freshly ground pepper to taste

1 to 2 tablespoons olive oil

2 loaves *Pan Cubano* (Cuban Bread; page 95) or French bread

⅓ to ½ cup mayonnaise

4 to 8 leaves iceberg or romaine lettuce

4 to 6 ripe plum tomatoes, thinly sliced

¼ cup finely chopped red onion

Salt and freshly ground black pepper to taste

Hearty steak sandwiches like this are standard fare at *loncherias* (lunch counters) in Miami and Tampa. Beef is harder to come by in Cuba, so in Havana a *pan con bistec* is a special treat.

Pound the steaks and marinate them with the garlic, lime juice, and salt and pepper for at least 30 minutes. Pat them dry with paper towels and brush them with the oil. Pan-fry the steaks in a hot skillet or grill them over hot coals for 2 to 3 minutes on each side, until browned and cooked to taste.

Trim the ends off the bread loaves, then cut the loaves into 6-inch sections. Split each section in half lengthwise and toast both sides lightly in the skillet or on the grill. Spread the cut sides with mayonnaise. Place lettuce on the bottom halves and add a layer of tomato slices. Sprinkle the tomatoes with onion, and season with salt and pepper. Place the steaks on top of the onion, and cover with the top pieces of bread.

SERVES 4.

# Elena Ruz
## Cuban Turkey Sandwich

This unusual turkey sandwich originated at El Carmelo, a popular late-night eatery in the Vedado neighborhood of Havana during the 1940s. It was invented by and named after Elena Ruz, a fashionable young lady who was a regular patron. The *Elena Ruz* has become a nostalgic favorite at Cuban sandwich shops in Miami. There are two versions of the sandwich. In one, it is made on good-quality, lightly toasted white sandwich bread, with crusts trimmed. In the other, the sandwich is made on trimmed but untoasted bread, then lightly pressed and toasted until golden in a croque monsieur iron. Though strawberry jam is traditional, guava jelly is a good and very Cuban alternative.

**8 slices good-quality white sandwich bread**
**3 ounces softened cream cheese**
**¼ cup strawberry jam or guava jelly**
**12 ounces thinly sliced roast turkey breast**

With a sharp knife, trim the crusts off the bread. Toast the bread lightly. Spread 4 of the slices evenly with the cream cheese, and the other slices with a thin layer of jam. Layer the turkey on the cream cheese side and place the remaining slices jam side down on top to close the sandwiches. Slice in half diagonally and serve.

SERVES 4.

# Fritas
## Cuban-Style Hamburgers

½ cup milk

1 cup fresh bread crumbs

½ cup finely chopped onion

1 large egg, lightly beaten

½ cup plus 2 tablespoons ketchup

2 teaspoons Worcestershire sauce

1 teaspoon salt

1 teaspoon mild paprika

¾ teaspoon ground cumin

¼ teaspoon freshly ground black pepper

1½ pounds lean ground beef

1 to 3 tablespoons olive oil

12 to 14 small hamburger rolls, split and lightly toasted

2 cups *Papas Cintas* (Shoestring Potatoes; below) or canned shoestring potatoes

It is hard to eat only one *frita*, and that's not just because they are small. These Cuban-style hamburgers are addictive! When hamburgers were first introduced to Cuba from the United States, Cubans found them a bit bland and "kicked it up a notch" by adding onion and other seasonings. Topping these tasty, three-bite burgers with freshly fried shoestring potatoes is another Cuban innovation that combines the flavors of a burger and fries in one compact package.

Place the milk and bread crumbs in a large mixing bowl. When the crumbs have absorbed most of the milk, mix in the egg, 2 tablespoons of the ketchup, the Worcestershire sauce, salt, paprika, cumin, and pepper. Add the ground beef and stir or knead the ingredients with clean hands until well combined. Use a ¼-cup measure to divide the burger mixture into 12 to 14 portions. Press the meat into patties about ½ inch thick and 3 inches in diameter. Fry the burgers in a hot, well-oiled skillet or grill them over hot coals for 2 to 4 minutes, until cooked to desired doneness. Place a *frita* on the bottom portion of each roll. Top each burger with a small bunch of *Papas Cintas* and a dollop of the remaining ketchup. Place the lids on the *fritas* and serve immediately.

MAKES 12 TO 14 BURGERS; SERVES 6 TO 8.

## Papas Cintas | Shoestring Potatoes

3 medium-size russet potatoes

Vegetable oil for deep-frying

Salt to taste

Peel and grate the potatoes using either the coarse grater blade of a food processor or the largest holes of a hand grater. As they are grated, place the potatoes in a bowl of cold, lightly salted water so they won't discolor. In a deep-fryer or deep, heavy skillet, heat at least 2 inches of oil to 375° F. Pat the potatoes dry with paper towels, then fry them in small batches until crisp and golden. As they are cooked, remove the potatoes with a slotted spatula, and drain on paper towels. Sprinkle lightly with salt. Keep the potatoes warm in a preheated 275° F. oven until ready to serve.

SERVES 4 TO 6; MAKES ENOUGH TO GARNISH 12 TO 14 FRITAS.

# Rosquillas de Papas
## Potato Doughnuts

2½ cups all-purpose flour

2 teaspoons baking powder

¾ teaspoon salt

½ teaspoon baking soda

¼ teaspoon ground cinnamon

⅓ cup milk

2 tablespoons dry sherry or white wine

1 large egg

2 tablespoons butter, melted

1 teaspoon pure vanilla extract

½ cup mashed potatoes

1½ cups sugar

Vegetable oil for deep-frying

To supplement her family's income, Marita opened a small snack stand on a corner in a modest residential neighborhood in Havana. Over time, she has built up a clientele of regular customers who stop by each day to buy a *cafecito* or *refresco* and one of her home-made *rosquillas*.

These light, crisp doughnuts are leavened with baking powder, baking soda, and eggs. They are often made with mashed white potatoes, but other traditional Cuban root vegetables like yuca, *boniato*, and yam may substituted.

Sift together the flour, baking powder, salt, baking soda, and cinnamon. In a large measuring cup or mixing bowl, whisk together the milk, sherry, egg, butter, and vanilla. Put the potatoes in a large bowl and, using an electric mixer, beat the potatoes, gradually adding ¾ cup of the sugar. Alternately add the dry and liquid ingredients to the potatoes, stirring well after each addition. Stir to combine thoroughly, then let the dough rest for 15 minutes.

In a deep-fryer or a heavy, deep skillet, heat at least 2 inches of oil to 375° F. On a floured work surface, roll out the dough to a thickness of ½ inch. With a lightly floured doughnut cutter, cut out rings. Fry the *rosquillas* and the doughnut holes in small batches, turning once, until golden brown, 3 to 4 minutes. Drain on crumpled paper towels, then roll in the remaining sugar. They are best when eaten shortly after frying.

MAKES 18 TO 20 *ROSQUILLAS* AND 18 TO 20 DOUGHNUT HOLES.

# Empanaditas de Picadillo con Masa de Yuca
## Small Beef Empanadas with Yuca Crust

Yuca (also called cassava) is a starchy root vegetable that has been a Cuban staple since before Columbus arrived in 1492. The island's original indigenous inhabitants, the Ciboney and Taino Indians, included cooked yuca in their stews and made shredded, dried yuca into a crackerlike bread. Over the centuries, as Spanish and African influences were added to Cuban cooking, yuca has been used in many dishes. Like the potato, yuca makes a good base for bread and pastry doughs. Our friend Beatriz Llamas, a Spanish cookbook author who lives with her family in Havana, makes wonderful cocktail-size *empanaditas* with a yuca-based crust. She fills the versatile dough with either savory or sweet fillings.

**1 fresh yuca (about 1 pound), peeled and halved lengthwise**
**1/2 to 3/4 cup all-purpose flour**
**1 tablespoon butter, softened**
**1 large egg yolk**
**1/4 teaspoon salt**
**1 cup *Picadillo Clásico* (Beef Picadillo; page 78)**
**Vegetable oil for deep-frying**

Place the yuca in a large saucepan with enough cold water to cover by 2 inches. Bring the water to a boil over high heat. Reduce the heat to medium and cook the yuca, uncovered, until it swells and becomes tender, 20 to 30 minutes. Drain the yuca and remove and discard the fibrous core. Mash by passing the yuca through either a food mill or a sieve. Lightly dust a work surface with flour and place 1 cup of the puree on top. Make a well in the center of the puree and put in the flour, butter, egg yolk, and salt. Knead until all the ingredients are well combined. The mixture should not be sticky. If the dough sticks to your fingers, gradually knead in additional flour, 1 tablespoon at a time.

Roll out the dough on a lightly floured surface as thinly as possible. With a sharp cutter, cut out circles 4 inches in diameter; set aside.

Place a rounded teaspoon of picadillo on one side of each of the circles of dough without letting it reach the edges. Moisten the edges of the circles with water. Fold the dough over to form a half circle and press the edges together lightly with the tines of a fork to seal the *empanaditas* closed.

Heat at least 2 inches of oil in a deep-fryer or a very heavy, deep skillet to 375° F. Preheat the oven to 275° F. Fry the *empanaditas*, 2 or 3 at a time, until golden brown, 3 to 4 minutes, turning occasionally with a slotted spoon. Drain on paper towels and keep warm on a baking sheet in the oven until ready to serve.

MAKES ABOUT 15 EMPANADAS; SERVES 4 TO 6.

# Empanadas de Espinacas Café Versailles
## Spinach Empanadas Café Versailles

**FOR THE DOUGH**

2 cups all-purpose flour

1 teaspoon baking powder

½ teaspoon salt

1 teaspoon sugar

4 tablespoons lard or vegetable
   shortening

2 tablespoons butter

1 large whole egg

1 large egg yolk

**FOR THE FILLING**

2 tablespoons butter or olive oil

¼ cup finely chopped onion

2 tablespoons flour

1 cup milk

1¼ cups grated fontina or Swiss cheese

1 (10-ounce) package frozen spinach,
   thawed

Salt and freshly ground black pepper to
   taste

Freshly grated nutmeg to taste

About ¼ cup flour for the work surface

Lard or vegetable oil for deep-frying;
   or 1 egg, beaten together with
   1 tablespoon water, if baking

Café Versailles is a popular gathering place for Cuban Americans in Miami. Open from 8 A.M. to 2 A.M. Sunday through Thursday and until 3:30 A.M. on Friday and 4:30 A.M. on Saturday, this lively establishment is made up of an elegant restaurant, a bakery and coffee shop, and a stand-up outdoor coffee bar, where businessmen get together for a quick *café Cubano*. Empanadas are a popular snack sold both at the coffee bar and the bakery.

Make the dough: In a large mixing bowl, thoroughly combine the flour, baking powder, salt, and sugar. With a pastry blender or two knives, cut the lard and butter into the flour mixture until it resembles coarse cornmeal. Make a well in the middle of the flour mixture. Place the whole egg and egg yolk in the well. Use an electric mixer or a fork and your hands to mix in the egg and enough cold water (about ½ cup) to make a soft, smooth, pliable dough. Place the dough in a bowl, cover, and refrigerate for at least 30 minutes.

While the dough is chilling, make the filling: In a large saucepan over medium heat, melt the butter. Add the onion and sauté until softened, 2 to 3 minutes. Stir in the flour and cook, stirring, for 1 minute. Whisk in the milk and ¾ cup of the cheese. Cook, stirring, until the sauce thickens. Squeeze any excess moisture out of the spinach, then stir the spinach into the sauce. Fold in the remaining cheese. Taste and season with salt, pepper, and nutmeg.

Lightly flour a work surface. Divide the dough into 6 to 8 balls. Return all but one ball to the refrigerator. Roll the ball into a circle about ⅛ inch thick. Put 3 to 4 tablespoons of the filling in the middle of the dough circle. Brush the edges of the circle lightly with water. Fold the dough over to make a half circle. Trim the edges with a pizza wheel to make a neat half-moon shape. Press down with the tines of a fork to seal the edge. Continue to make empanadas until all of the dough balls and filling are used.

To fry the empanadas: In a deep-fryer or a deep, heavy skillet, heat enough lard to cover the empanadas completely to 365 to 375° F. Working in small batches to maintain the lard temperature, lower the empanadas into the hot fat. Fry, turning once or twice, until the empanadas are golden brown, 4 to 6 minutes. Remove and drain on crumpled paper towels.

To bake the empanadas: Preheat the oven to 350° F. Place the empanadas on a baking sheet lined with baking parchment or aluminum foil. Brush the tops with the egg wash. Bake until golden brown, 20 to 30 minutes Serve the empanadas hot or at room temperature.

MAKES 6 TO 8 EMPANADAS; SERVES 4 TO 6.

# Pastel de Pollo
## Chicken Pie

### FOR THE FILLING

**2 to 3 clove. garlic**

**1 teaspoon salt**

**½ teaspoon ground cumin**

**¼ teaspoon freshly ground black pepper**

**⅛ teaspoon ground cinnamon**

**½ cup fresh bitter orange juice, or**
**¼ cup regular orange juice and ¼ cup**
**fresh lime juice**

**1½ pounds boneless, skinless chicken**
**breasts**

**¼ to ⅓ cup olive oil**

**1½ cups chopped onion**

**1 cup diced green bell pepper**

**1 cup tomato sauce**

**1 cup dry sherry or white wine**

**2 tablespoons brine-packed capers,**
**drained**

**⅓ cup sliced pimiento-stuffed green**
**olives**

**⅓ cup raisins**

**⅓ cup toasted slivered almonds**

### FOR THE CRUST

**2¼ cups all-purpose flour**

**¾ teaspoon salt**

**1½ teaspoons baking powder**

**1½ tablespoons sugar**

**1 (12-ounce) package cream cheese,**
**softened**

**¾ cup (1½ sticks) unsalted butter,**
**softened**

**1 large egg, beaten (optional)**

F or parties and saint's days, Cuban Americans often order a *pastel de pollo* from their neighborhood bakery or grocery store to serve as part of a festive buffet. It is also sold by the slice at Cuban cafés and bakeries. I like to serve this intriguing sweet and savory pie as the entrée for a light lunch accompanied by a green salad and a glass of chilled white wine.

Make the filling: Crush the garlic in a garlic press. With a fork, mash the garlic, together with the salt, cumin, pepper, and cinnamon, to a paste. Stir the garlic paste into the bitter orange juice. Place the chicken breasts in a large glass mixing bowl and pour the marinade over them. Cover and refrigerate for at least 1 hour. Remove the chicken and pat it dry with paper towels. Reserve the marinade.

Heat the oil in a large, heavy skillet over medium heat and add the chicken; cook for 4 to 5 minutes, until browned on both sides. Stir in the onion and bell pepper and sauté over medium-low heat until the onion is translucent, about 3 minutes. Stir in the tomato sauce, sherry, capers, olives, raisins, and the reserved marinade. Cover the pan, reduce the heat, and simmer for 30 minutes.

Remove the filling from the heat and let it cool while you make the crust. When cool, remove chicken, shred into bite-sized pieces, and return it to sauce.

Make the crust: Sift the flour, then sift it again with the salt, baking powder, and sugar. Set aside. In a large bowl, use an electric mixer to combine the cream cheese and butter until well blended. Gradually add the flour mixture and beat until smooth.

Divide the dough into 2 equal balls. Place each on a floured square of waxed paper and roll it into a circle about ¼ inch thick and 13½ inches in diameter. Cover each round with another sheet of waxed paper and refrigerate for at least 30 minutes.

Preheat the oven to 425° F.

Place one circle of the dough in a 10-inch pie pan so that 1 inch of the dough hangs over the sides and spoon in the filling. Sprinkle with almonds. Top the filling with the second circle of dough. Fold the edges together and seal with the tines of a fork. Make a few slashes in the top crust for steam to escape. If you like a shiny crust, brush the top with beaten egg.

Bake for 10 minutes. Lower the oven temperature to 350° F. and continue baking for 30 to 40 minutes more, until the crust is golden. Serve warm.

SERVES 6.

# Pastel de Medianoche
## Midnight Pie

This unusual layered pie is an elegant variation on the *medianoche* sandwich, which includes the same basic filling served on egg bread and toasted on a sandwich grill. Savory pies are often sold by the slice at Cuban bakeries and may also be ordered whole as takeout party food. This one cuts beautifully when cold, and makes a great midnight supper when served with a green salad and a glass of wine.

Preheat the oven to 375° F.

In a mixing bowl, combine the flour, sugar, baking powder, salt, and nutmeg. Add the butter and cut it into the flour mixture with a pastry blender or your fingertips until the mixture resembles coarse crumbs. Add the egg yolks and the whole egg, wine, and 2 tablespoons water. Stir with a fork until the dough comes together, adding additional water by tablespoonfuls until the dough comes together. Knead lightly. Divide the dough into 2 equal portions and roll out each portion into a round about ⅓ inch thick. Butter a 9-inch deep-dish pie pan and line it with one of the dough rounds. Spread the dough with the mustard and cover with layers of ham, cheese, *puerco asado*, turkey, more cheese, and pickle slices. Cover with the second dough round and trim, seal, and flute the edges.

To make the glaze, combine the egg yolk and milk; brush the top of the pie with the glaze. Using a sharp knife, make a few slits in the top to allow steam to escape. If desired, decorate the top of the pie with pastry-dough cutouts of a crescent moon and stars. Bake the pie until golden, 40 to 50 minutes. Serve chilled or at room temperature.

SERVES 6 TO 8.

2½ cups all-purpose flour

2 tablespoons sugar

2 teaspoons baking powder

½ teaspoon salt

¼ teaspoon freshly grated nutmeg

½ cup (1 stick) unsalted butter

2 large egg yolks plus 1 whole large egg, beaten

⅓ cup dry sherry or white wine

1 to 2 tablespoons yellow or Dijon-style mustard

⅓ pound smoked ham, thinly sliced

½ pound Swiss cheese, thinly sliced

⅓ pound *Puerco Asado* (Roast Pork Loin; page 53), thinly sliced

⅓ pound roast turkey breast, thinly sliced

6 to 8 long thin slices dill pickle

FOR THE GLAZE

1 large egg yolk

1 tablespoon milk

# Pizza de Chorizo y Cebolla
## Chorizo and Onion Pizza

By 11 A.M., people in Havana have begun to gather in front of the outdoor pizza stand of Juan Carlos and his daughter Olga Lidia. The tantalizing aroma of hot fresh pizza draws hungry apartment dwellers from a nearby complex. The pizza craze in Cuba, as Juan Carlos explains, began in the 1950s with the opening in Havana of Montecatini, a pizza parlor named after the famous Italian resort city. For Juan Carlos, who was a teenager at the time, going to Montecatini was a great treat. He began to help out at the pizza parlor and learned how to make his new favorite food. "Pizza," he says, "is the perfect snack food for people on the go, delicious, economical, and quick enough to make fresh to order. Once you have the base, the only limit to the kinds of pizza you can make is your own imagination."

In her small, simple kitchen set-up, Olga makes individual crisp, thin-crusted pies to order. The choices today are chorizo, onion, and cheese; ham, onion, and cheese; or plain cheese. As they are ready, she grips the edges of the piping-hot pizzas with small sheets of brown butcher paper and hands them to the waiting customers. The customers, in turn, fold their pizzas in half like a turnover and walk off eating them out of hand.

Make the dough: In a small bowl, combine the yeast with the sugar and 1 cup warm water. In a large mixing bowl, stir together 2½ cups of the flour and the salt. When the yeast begins to foam, make a well in the middle of the flour mixture and pour in the yeast mixture and 2 tablespoons of the oil. With a your hands or a wooden spatula, combine the wet and dry ingredients. Knead the mixture, gradually adding more flour, if needed, until the dough is smooth and elastic. Divide the dough into 4 to 6 equal portions.

Generously oil 4 to 6 metal pie pans, 8 to 9 inches in diameter. Roll out the portions of dough into rounds about ¼ inch thick and large enough to line the bottoms of the pans. Place the dough rounds in the pans and cover the pans with clean kitchen towels. Set aside in a warm, draft-free area to rise for 30 to 40 minutes.

Top the pizzas: Preheat the oven to 425° F. Spread about 2 tablespoons of the tomato sauce on each dough round. Add a layer of chorizo and a layer of onion. Top with 2 to 3 more tablespoons of tomato sauce and about ½ cup of the cheese.

Bake the pizzas on the middle shelves of the oven until the crust is golden brown and the topping is hot and bubbling, about 15 minutes.

SERVES 4 TO 6.

FOR THE DOUGH

1 (¼-ounce) package fast-rising (instant) yeast

½ teaspoon sugar

2½ to 3 cups all-purpose flour

½ teaspoon salt

¼ cup olive oil

FOR THE TOPPING

1 (15-ounce) can tomato sauce

10 ounces Spanish chorizo or hard salami, thinly sliced

1 large or 2 small sweet yellow onions, peeled and thinly sliced

2 to 2½ cups shredded fontina, Colby, or Monterey Jack cheese

# Croquetas de Pollo
## Chicken Croquettes

2 cups chicken broth

½ onion, peeled, plus 1 cup minced onion

1 pound boneless, skinless chicken breasts, or 3 cups chopped cooked chicken or turkey

4 tablespoons unsalted butter

¾ cup plus ⅓ cup all-purpose flour

¾ cup half-and-half or milk

¼ teaspoon freshly grated nutmeg

Salt and freshly ground black pepper to taste

1 tablespoon minced fresh parsley (optional)

3 or 4 large eggs, beaten

2 cups dry bread crumbs

Croquettes are classic Cuban street food, economical, satisfying, and versatile. Chicken is rationed in Cuba—one pound of chicken per person per month—but it goes a lot further when you make croquettes.

In a 1½- to 2-quart saucepan, bring the broth and ½ onion to a simmer. If using raw chicken breasts, add them to the broth and poach gently until cooked through, about 5 minutes. Place the poached chicken (or chopped cooked chicken, if using) in a food processor with a steel knife blade. Pulse 2 or 3 times, until the chicken is finely chopped, but not pureed. Set aside. Strain the broth and set it aside; discard the onion.

In a large saucepan, melt the butter over medium heat. Add the minced onion and cook, stirring often, until softened and translucent, 3 to 4 minutes. Gradually stir in the ⅓ cup flour to make a paste. Whisk in ¾ cup of the reserved broth and the half-and-half. Cook, stirring, until the sauce is smooth and thick, 3 to 5 minutes. Add the nutmeg and season with salt and pepper. Fold in the chicken and the parsley, if using. Taste and adjust the seasonings. Spread the chicken mixture into a shallow baking pan and chill in the freezer or refrigerator until firm, about 30 minutes.

While the chicken mixture is chilling, in a mixing bowl, beat the eggs together with 1½ to 2 tablespoons water. Place the ¾ cup flour on a plate or small platter. Place the bread crumbs in a shallow baking dish. Shape heaping tablespoons of the chicken mixture into cylinders about ¾ inch thick and 2½ inches long. Dip the croquettes first in the flour, then in the eggs, and then roll them in the bread crumbs. As they are coated, place the croquettes on a baking sheet and refrigerate until all of the chicken mixture is used. Cover the croquettes and chill for at least 30 minutes to hold the shape and make the coating adhere. The croquettes may also be covered and frozen at this point for up to 2 weeks.

Preheat the oven to 250° F. In a deep-fryer or a deep, heavy skillet, heat at least 2 inches of oil to 360 to 375° F. Add the croquettes in small batches and fry, turning occasionally, until golden brown, 3 to 4 minutes. Remove them with a slotted spoon or spatula and drain or baking sheets lined with crumpled paper towels. To keep the croquettes warm as you fry them, move the baking sheet to the oven. Serve warm.

MAKES 18 TO 20 CROQUETTES; SERVES 4 TO 6 AS AN ENTRÉE OR 8 TO 10 AS AN APPETIZER.

# Croquetas de Jamón
## Ham Croquettes

I first developed a taste for *croquetas* during the years I lived in Madrid and was delighted to find that they are just as popular in Cuba. Making croquettes is an elegant way to generously feed a crowd with a small amount of cooked meat or seafood. From Havana to Miami, ham *croquetas* are a favorite snack or light lunch. They are often sold at snack bars and Cuban bakeries.

In a 3-quart heavy-bottomed saucepan, melt the butter over medium-low heat. Add the onion and cook, stirring often, until softened and translucent, 3 to 5 minutes. Gradually whisk in the ⅓ cup flour, stirring until smooth. Gradually whisk in the milk and continue to cook, stirring, until the sauce is quite thick. Whisk in the cheese, if using, and nutmeg. Fold in the ham and parsley. Season the mixture with salt and pepper. Spread the ham mixture into a shallow baking dish and place in the refrigerator or freezer until well chilled.

In a mixing bowl, beat the eggs together with 1½ to 2 tablespoons water. Place the ½ cup flour on a plate or small platter. Place the bread crumbs in a shallow baking dish and season them with salt and pepper. Shape heaping tablespoons of the ham mixture into cylinders about ¾ inch thick and 2½ inches long. Dip the croquettes first in the flour, then in the eggs, and then roll them in the bread crumbs. As they are coated, place the croquettes on a baking sheet and refrigerate until all of the ham mixture is used. Cover the croquettes and chill for at least 30 minutes. This will help them to hold their shape and make the coating adhere. The croquettes may also be covered and frozen at this point for up to 2 weeks.

Preheat the oven to 250° F. In a deep-fryer or a deep, heavy skillet, heat at least 2 inches of oil to 360 to 375° F. Add the croquettes in small batches and fry, turning occasionally, until golden brown, 3 to 4 minutes. Remove them with a slotted spoon or spatula and drain or baking sheets lined with crumpled paper towels. To keep the croquettes warm as you fry them, move the baking sheet to the oven. Serve warm.

MAKES 18 TO 20 CROQUETTES; SERVES 4 TO 6 AS AN ENTRÉE OR 8 TO 10 AS AN APPETIZER.

**4 tablespoons unsalted butter**

**1 cup finely chopped onion**

**½ cup plus ⅓ cup all-purpose flour**

**1½ cups milk**

**¼ cup freshly grated Parmesan cheese (optional)**

**¼ teaspoon freshly grated nutmeg**

**3 cups finely chopped ham**

**2 tablespoons minced fresh flat-leaf parsley**

**Salt and freshly ground black pepper to taste**

**3 or 4 large eggs, beaten**

**1½ to 2½ cups fresh or dried bread crumbs**

**Vegetable oil for deep-frying**

# Frituras de Malanga Cruda
## Raw Taro Root Fritters

1 pound (2 to 3) fresh *malangas* (taro
   roots)

2 to 3 teaspoons minced fresh cilantro
   or flat-leaf parsley

2 teaspoons fresh lime or lemon juice

1½ teaspoons minced garlic (1 clove)

1 large egg, lightly beaten

½ teaspoon salt

¼ teaspoon freshly ground black pepper

Vegetable oil for deep-frying

Taro root was brought to Cuba by African slaves and quickly incorporated into Cuban cooking. There are two main varieties, brown-skinned, white-fleshed taro and a yellow-fleshed variety. Taro must be peeled and cooked before eating. It has a flavor and texture similar to a white potato and when boiled it turns a grayish color.

Fritters are usually made with grated fresh *malanga*. Though it is sometimes finely grated to make almost a paste, I prefer to use the coarser holes of the grater to make delicate lacey fritters that resemble little crabs or starfish. Some of the crispest and tastiest *malanga* fritters we had in Cuba were served as an appetizer at Paladar Vista Mar, a low-key but elegant restaurant in the Miramar neighborhood of Havana.

Preheat the oven to 275° F.

Peel the *malangas* and grate them using either the large or medium holes of the grater. In a mixing bowl, stir together the grated *malangas*, cilantro, lime juice, garlic, egg, salt, and pepper.

In a deep-fryer or a deep, heavy skillet, heat at least 2 inches of oil to 365 to 375° F. Working in batches of 3 or 4 fritters, drop the *malanga* batter by teaspoonfuls (for appetizers) or tablespoonfuls (for a side dish) into the hot oil. Fry, turning, if necessary, with a slotted spoon, until the fritters are golden brown, 3 to 4 minutes. Drain on paper towels, and keep warm in the oven until all of the batter has been fried. Serve hot.

Fritters are best when served immediately, but we have found that these may be frozen for up to 2 weeks and reheated in a 350° F. oven for about 15 minutes, with good results.

MAKES 12 TO 16 FRITTERS; SERVES 4 TO 6 AS A SIDE DISH OR 6 TO 8 AS AN APPETIZER.

# Frituras de Maíz Dulce
## Sweet Corn Fritters

Corn, a gift to Cuban cooking from the island's early Taino inhabitants, makes wonderfully delicate fritters. The sweet fritters here are a delicious snack to eat with a cup of coffee or hot chocolate. To make a savory version, reduce the sugar to 1 tablespoon, add 2 tablespoons finely minced onion, omit the aniseed and powdered sugar, and increase the salt to 1 teaspoon.

In a mixing bowl, combine the corn puree, egg, sugar, aniseed, and salt. Sift the flour and baking powder together into the corn mixture and stir to make a batter. In a deep-fryer or a deep, heavy skillet, heat at least 2 inches of oil to 375° F. Drop the batter by tablespoonfuls into the hot oil. Fry, turning the fritters with a slotted spoon, until golden brown, 3 to 4 minutes. Drain on paper towels, dust with powdered sugar, and serve immediately.

MAKES 16 TO 18 FRITTERS; SERVES 4 TO 6.

1 cup pureed fresh or frozen corn kernels
1 large egg, lightly beaten
5 tablespoons sugar
½ teaspoon aniseed
½ teaspoon salt
½ cup all-purpose flour
½ teaspoon baking powder
Vegetable oil for deep-frying
Powdered sugar

# Mariquitas
## Fried Plantain Chips

2 large green plantains

Vegetable oil for deep-frying

Salt to taste, preferably kosher or sea
salt

*Mojo Criollo* (Cuban Garlic Sauce; page
48)

**S**top by most any Cuban takeout window or *loncheria* and you'll see people buying brown paper cones filled with *mariquitas*, also called *chicharritas*. These wafer-thin slices of green plantain are deep-fried until crisp and golden, then sprinkled with salt. Whether sliced crosswise like potato chips or lengthwise, they are delicious either eaten as is or sprinkled with tart, garlicky *mojo*.

Peel the plantains: Cut off both ends, then cut slits through the skin, being careful not to cut the flesh. Peel off the skin. Using a mandolin set on the "thin" setting, slice the plantains lengthwise. If not frying immediately, place the slices in cold acidulated water. When ready to fry, pat the slices dry thoroughly with paper towels.

In a deep-fryer or a large, deep skillet, heat at least 2 inches of oil to 375° F. Working in batches, carefully add the plantain slices to the oil. Fry, turning occasionally, until crisp and golden brown, 1 to 2 minutes. Drain on crumpled paper towels and sprinkle with salt. Serve immediately, with *Mojo Criollo* if desired.

**SERVES 4 TO 6.**

# Papas Rellenas
## Meat-Stuffed Potatoes

**2 pounds baking potatoes (Idaho or russet)**

**Salt to taste**

**½ cup (1 stick) butter**

**2 (3-ounce) packages cream cheese**

**Freshly ground black pepper to taste (optional)**

**2 cups *Picadillo Clásico* (Beef Picadillo; page 78)**

**3 or 4 large eggs**

**1 cup all-purpose flour**

**2 to 3 cups bread crumbs**

**Vegetable oil for deep-frying**

**D**eep-fried stuffed potatoes are a popular snack throughout Latin America. As the lunch hour approaches, people gather at the takeout window of the small *paladar* that Justo and his wife, Rosario, run out of the front of their modest house in a residential area of Havana. Justo, who also works as the cook on a ship, is sometimes out at sea for months at a time, but when he is at home you will find him here in the kitchen. When he is gone, Rosario, who is also a great cook, takes over. *Papas rellenas* are one of the specialties of the house.

Peel and quarter the potatoes and place them in a large saucepan with enough water to cover. Add 1 to 2 teaspoons salt and bring to a gentle boil. Cook the potatoes until tender when pierced with a knife, about 20 minutes. Drain the potatoes and mash them together with the butter and cream cheese. Season the mashed potatoes with salt and pepper to taste. Refrigerate the mashed potatoes until cooled and firm enough to shape with your hands.

Scoop about ¼ cup of the potato mixture into the cupped palm of your hand and use the fingers of your other hand to form it into a shallow bowl shape. Place a rounded tablespoon of the *Picadillo Clásico* in the hollow and press down on it with your fingertips. Mold the sides up over the filling to enclose it. If necessary, add a little more potato mixture to enclose the filling completely. Repeat until all the potato mixture and filling have been used. Use both hands to shape the stuffed potatoes into balls. As you finish them, place the shaped potato balls on a baking pan and refrigerate until ready to deep-fry.

In a shallow bowl, beat the eggs together with 3 to 4 tablespoons water. Roll the potato balls in the flour, and gently shake off any excess. Dip them into the eggs and then roll them in the bread crumbs until they are evenly coated.

Preheat the oven to 300° F. Line a large baking sheet with slightly crumpled paper towels.

In a deep-fryer or a large, deep skillet, heat at least 2 inches of oil to 375° F. Using a slotted spoon, gently lower a stuffed and breaded potato roll into the hot oil. Fry one at a time, using the spoon to gently turn it, until golden brown on all sides, 2 to 3 minutes. As they are fried, transfer the potato rolls to the baking sheet to drain. Keep them warm in the oven until all are cooked, then serve hot. These may be prepared and fried in advance, then frozen for up to 1 month. To serve, reheat in a 350° F. oven for about 30 minutes, until crisp and hot.

**MAKES 14 TO 16 STUFFED POTATOES; SERVES 6 TO 8.**

# Cebollas Encurtidas
## Pickled Onions

2 large red onions, or 1 red and 1 white, peeled and thinly sliced

1 cup cider or distilled white vinegar

1 teaspoon salt

1 teaspoon ground allspice

1 teaspoon dried oregano leaves, preferably Mexican oregano

3 bay leaves

½ teaspoon black peppercorns

1 fresh habanero or jalapeño chile, seeded and sliced (optional)

Pickled onions are wonderful in salads, and great as a garnish for many other Cuban dishes. They are so tasty that I have been known to snack on them right out of the refrigerator.

Place the onions in a saucepan and add cold water to cover. Bring to a boil over medium-high heat. Immediately drain the onions thoroughly and place them in a glass bowl. Toss with the vinegar, salt, allspice, oregano, bay leaves, peppercorns, and chile, if using. Let macerate in the refrigerator for at least 1 day before serving. They will keep, refrigerated, up to 4 weeks.

MAKES ABOUT 1 QUART.

# Masitas de Puerco
## Crisp Fried Pork Chunks

At El Palacios de Los Jugos in Miami's Little Havana, crisp, juicy deep-fried chunks of pork are garnished with sliced onion and sold by the pound. *Masitas* are usually served with a side of rice and black beans.

Crush the garlic in a garlic press and place in a shallow, nonreactive baking dish. Add the oregano, salt, cumin, and pepper and mash together with a fork to make a paste. Stir in the bitter orange juice. Add the pork and toss to coat with the marinade. Cover and let the pork marinate, refrigerated, for at least 1 hour.

Preheat the oven to 275° F. In a deep-fryer or a deep, heavy skillet, heat at least 2 inches of oil to 375° F. Pat the pork dry with paper towels and fry it, a few chunks at a time, until crisp, golden brown, and cooked through, 4 to 5 minutes. Regulate the temperature as you add more pork to maintain an oil temperature between 350 and 375° F. Drain the pork on paper towels and keep warm in the oven. Garnish the pork with the *Cebollas Encurtidas* and lime wedges and serve hot.

SERVES 4 TO 6.

4 cloves garlic

1 teaspoon dried oregano leaves

1 teaspoon salt

½ teaspoon ground cumin

¼ teaspoon freshly ground black pepper

½ cup bitter orange juice, or ¼ cup regular orange juice and ¼ cup fresh lime juice

2 pounds boneless pork loin or shoulder, cut into 1½- to 2-inch cubes

Vegetable oil for deep-frying

1 cup *Cebollas Encurtidas* (Pickled Onions; opposite), or ½ large red onion, sliced into thin rings

Lime wedges

# Tamal en Hoja
## Fresh Corn Tamales

Tamales in Cuba can be traced back to the Ciboney, the original native inhabitants of the island. Cuban tamales are usually made with pureed fresh corn and, unlike Mexican tamales, the meat filling is often mixed in with the corn dough. In Cuba the corn used to make tamales is field (or dent) corn. It has a higher starch content than the sweet corn sold at grocery stores in the United States. When using sweet corn, it is usually necessary to add cornmeal or *masa harina* to the corn puree to thicken it.

Place the chorizo in a large, deep skillet over medium heat. Cook the chorizo until it begins to render its fat, 2 to 4 minutes. If there is not much rendered fat in the skillet, add 1 to 2 tablespoons oil. Add the pork and sauté until lightly browned and cooked through, 8 to 10 minutes. Remove the meats with a slotted spoon and set aside.

To the skillet, add the onion, bell pepper, and chiles and cook, stirring, until the onion is translucent, 3 to 5 minutes. Stir in the tomato sauce, wine, garlic, oregano, and cumin. Simmer over medium-low heat for 3 to 5 minutes, until the onion is transparent.

Return the meats to the skillet and continue to simmer, stirring occasionally, for an additional 5 minutes. Taste and season the mixture generously with salt and pepper. (If making the meat mixture in advance, refrigerate it until cool, then cover tightly and store in the refrigerator for 3 to 4 days or freeze for up to 1 month.)

If using fresh corn, remove and discard the husks and silk from the ears of corn. Using the large holes on a grater, grate the corn off the cobs into a mixing bowl. You should have 6 to 7 cups combined pulp and juice.

If using frozen corn, place the corn kernels in a food processor with a steel knife blade. Pulse until the corn is pureed.

Place the corn puree in a large saucepan and cook over low heat, stirring, for 5 minutes. Gradually stir in the cornmeal: start with ¾ cup; if it seems too thin, add more cornmeal, 1 teaspoon at a time. Continue to cook, stirring, until the corn mixture comes away from the sides of the pan when you stir.

Stir the meat mixture into the corn. Taste and adjust the seasonings. The mixture should be a bit salty, as salt will be leached out of the tamales as they boil. Place the tamale mixture in the refrigerator until it is cool.

*(continued)*

### Ingredients

½ pound Spanish chorizo or spicy dry salami, cut into ½-inch dice

1 to 3 tablespoons olive oil (optional)

1 pound pork loin or shoulder, cut into ¾-inch cubes

1½ cups chopped onion (1 medium)

1½ cups chopped green bell pepper (1 large)

2 to 3 *ajies cachucha*, or ½ to 1 jalapeño, seeded and minced (optional)

1 can (8-ounce) can tomato sauce

¼ cup white wine, or 2 tablespoons white wine vinegar

1½ tablespoons minced garlic (3 to 4 cloves)

1 teaspoon dried oregano leaves, crumbled

1 teaspoon ground cumin

Salt to taste

Freshly ground black pepper to taste (optional)

12 large ears fresh yellow corn, or 3 (1-pound) packages frozen corn kernels

¾ to 1 cup finely ground yellow cornmeal or *masa harina*

1 (8-ounce) package dried corn husks

Rinse about 50 corn husks and place them on paper towels to drain. Arrange two corn husks with the wide ends overlapping by about 2 inches. Place a third smaller husk on top to cover the overlap. Spoon ½ cup of the tamale mixture on top of the third husk. Fold in the long sides to cover the filling. Fold up the two pointed ends to form a rectangular package and tie with strips of corn husk (see Note) or kitchen string. Continue to form tamales until all of the mixture and husks have been used; you should have 14 to 16 tamales. Place the tamales in a large pot of boiling water. Boil gently for 60 minutes, adjusting the heat and adding more boiling water if needed. Serve the tamales hot, in their husk wrapping.

Note: To make corn-husk strings: Cut a ½-inch strip the length of a corn husk. Tie a knot at the narrowest end of the strip. Starting at the wider end, cut down the length of the strip in the middle almost to the knot. You should now have a ¼-inch-wide strip, double the length of the corn husk.

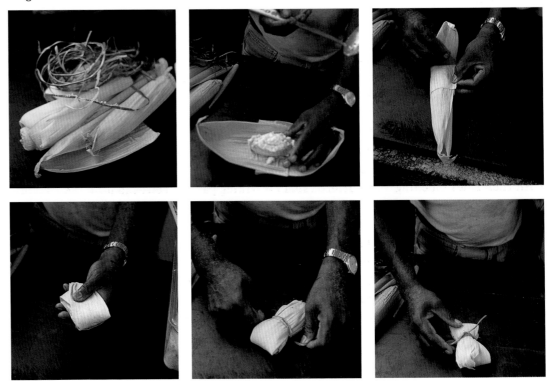

# Pan de Gloria
## Heavenly Cuban Sweet Rolls

**P**an de gloria, light, fluffy sweet rolls dusted with sugar, are standard fare at coffee kiosks in Cuba. Though they are not difficult to make, most of the Cubans we met bought them at the coffee window or at the bakery.

In a large mixing bowl, stir together 1 cup of the flour, the yeast, sugar, and salt. In a saucepan, combine the evaporated milk with enough water to make 2 cups total liquid. Stir in the oil and heat the liquids until very warm, 120 and 130° F. Make a well in the dry ingredients and pour in the warm liquids and the vanilla. Stir with a wooden spoon until well combined. Cover and set the mixture aside to rest in warm, draft-free area for 10 minutes.

Gradually mix in enough of the remaining flour (using the wooden spoon and then kneading with your hands) to make a smooth, slightly sticky dough. Form into a rough round and place in a large buttered bowl. Cover the bowl and set aside in a warm, draft-free area until doubled in size, 45 minutes to 1 hour. Turn the dough out onto a lightly floured work surface and knead briefly, until elastic and easy to handle, 3 to 5 minutes.

To make round rolls: Pinch off round portions of dough about the size of golf balls and place them, with their sides touching, in two buttered 9-inch round cake pans.

To make cinnamon pinwheel rolls: Divide the dough in half. Roll out one portion on a lightly floured surface into about a 12-inch square, about ½ inch thick. Brush the dough with butter and sprinkle with the cinnamon-sugar mixture. Roll up the dough and, using a sharp knife, slice the roll into pinwheels about 1 inch thick. Place the rolls cut side up, with their sides touching, in a buttered shallow baking pan. Roll out and form the remaining dough in the same manner. Cover the formed rolls and set aside to rise in a warm, draft-free area until doubled in size, 45 minutes to 1 hour.

Preheat the oven to 350° F. Bake the rolls for 20 to 25 minutes, until they are golden on top and sound slightly hollow when you tap them gently. While still warm, brush the rolls with melted butter and sprinkle with sugar or cinnamon sugar, or brush with honey or sugar syrup.

An alternative is to deep-fry the round rolls like doughnuts in oil heated to 365° F. until golden brown on all sides, 2 to 3 minutes. Drain on paper towels, then roll in sugar or cinnamon sugar while still warm.

MAKES 28 TO 30 ROLLS.

4 to 5 cups all-purpose flour

2 (¼-ounce) packages fast-rising (instant) yeast

⅓ cup sugar

1½ teaspoons salt

1 (5-ounce) can evaporated milk

⅓ cup mild vegetable oil

2 teaspoons pure vanilla extract

TO FORM THE ROLLS

¼ to ½ cup butter, melted

1 tablespoon ground cinnamon combined with ¾ cup sugar (optional)

Granulated sugar for dusting, or honey or sugar syrup (see page 176) for drizzling

# Pastelitos de Coco
## Tiny Coconut Turnovers

**FOR THE DOUGH**

2¼ cups all-purpose flour

1½ tablespoons sugar

1½ teaspoons baking powder

¾ teaspoon salt

1 (12-ounce) package cream cheese, softened

¾ cup (1½ sticks) unsalted butter, softened

**FOR THE FILLING**

½ (17-ounce) can grated coconut in heavy syrup

1 large egg white, beaten together with 1 tablespoon water

¼ cup sugar

These sweet, delicate little pastries are the perfect complement to a strong, flavorful cup of *café Cubano*. Grated coconut in heavy syrup, which is sold in cans at many Latin American grocery stores, makes these tiny turnovers a snap to make.

Make the dough: Sift the flour, then sift it again with the sugar, baking powder, and salt. Set aside. In a large bowl, use a heavy-duty electric mixer to combine the cream cheese and butter until well blended. Gradually add the flour mixture and stir until thoroughly incorporated. Turn the dough out onto a lightly floured surface and knead until smooth. Cover the dough and refrigerate for at least 30 minutes.

Preheat the oven to 425° F. Line baking sheets with baking parchment.

Roll the dough out as thinly as possible. Using a 3-inch biscuit cutter, cut out circles of dough. Brush the edges with water. Place 1 scant teaspoon of the coconut on one side of each dough circle and fold the other side over to make a turnover. Press the edges with the tines of a fork to seal. Place the *pastelitos* on the prepared baking sheets. Brush the tops lightly with the egg-white mixture and sprinkle with the sugar. Bake for 8 to 9 minutes, until barely golden. Allow to cool on a rack; serve at room temperature.

**MAKES ABOUT 3 DOZEN *PASTELITOS*.**

# Torticas de Morón
## Cuban Shortbread Cookies

3 cups all-purpose flour

1½ teaspoons baking powder

¾ to 1 teaspoon ground cinnamon, or to taste

½ teaspoon salt

8 ounces lard or vegetable shortening

⅔ cup granulated sugar

2 teaspoons finely grated orange zest

1½ to 2 teaspoons aniseed (optional)

1 large egg, beaten

2 tablespoons orange juice concentrate

1 tablespoon rum, or 1 teaspoon pure vanilla extract

¼ cup powdered sugar (optional)

3 to 4 tablespoons guava jelly or jam (optional)

These shortbread cookies are a typical recipe from the town of Morón in the Cuban province of Ciego de Ávila. They are sold at bakeries both in Cuba and in the United States and are a favorite snack to consume with a *cafecito*. Though some contemporary recipes call for vegetable shortening or even oil, it is lard that gives these cookies their wonderfully delicate texture. Contrary to popular belief, lard ranks with butter in digestibility and is actually lower in saturated fat than butter.

Preheat oven to 350° F. Line a baking sheet with baking parchment.

Sift together the flour, baking powder, cinnamon, and salt. Stir the flour mixture, making sure the dry ingredients are well combined.

In a large mixing bowl, use an electric mixer to beat the lard until fluffy. Add the granulated sugar and continue beating until the mixture is creamy and light. Add the orange zest, aniseed, and egg, continuing to beat until well combined. Add the orange juice concentrate and rum and mix well. Beat half of the dry ingredients into the lard mixture, then continue to add the dry ingredients ½ cup at a time, beating until the dough is stiff and forms a smooth ball.

On a floured surface, roll out the dough to a thickness of ½ inch. Using a round cutter about 2 inches in diameter, cut the dough into circles and arrange them on the prepared baking sheet. With a sewing thimble or your finger, make a small depression in the center of each cookie. Bake the *torticas* on the middle rack of the oven until light golden brown, 10 to 12 minutes. Let the cookies cool on the baking sheet for 5 minutes, then transfer them to a rack to cool. Sprinkle the cooled *torticas* lightly with powdered sugar and fill the depressions in the centers with small dollops of jelly, if desired. These cookies freeze well. If freezing, dust them with sugar and fill with jelly just before serving.

MAKES ABOUT 3 DOZEN *TORTICAS*.

# Masa Real de Guayaba
## Guava Tart

Guava is a popular filling for sweet tarts and turnovers in Cuba. Most bakeries and coffee stands sell *masa real de guayaba*, in which slices of guava paste are sandwiched between 2 layers of egg-rich dough in a shallow rectangular baking dish. The tart is cut into squares like double-crusted bar cookies that are convenient to sell individually.

Cheese—either a sharp variety like manchego or Cheddar, or cream cheese—often accompanies guava desserts. The unusual cream cheese ice cream on page 157 is delicious with this tart.

Preheat the oven to 350° F. Butter and lightly flour a 9- to 10-inch round or square false-bottomed tart or cake pan.

Sift together the flour, baking powder, and salt. With an electric mixer, cream the butter and granulated sugar and mix in the egg. Gradually beat in the flour mixture, alternating with 1 tablespoon cold water and the vanilla, to form a stiff dough. Gather the dough into a mass; divide it in half and form it into 2 balls. If not using immediately, wrap each ball tightly in plastic wrap and refrigerate.

On a lightly floured surface, roll one of the dough balls into a circle or square large enough to line the prepared pan. Carefully roll the dough up on the rolling pin and unroll it into the pan, pressing it gently into the bottom and against the sides. Cover the bottom of the tart with the guava slices.

Roll out the remaining dough ball into a round or square about 1/4 inch thick and large enough to cover the top of the tart. For a plain top crust, roll the dough up on a rolling pin and unroll it on top of the guava. Trim the edges with kitchen scissors or a sharp knife.

For a more decorative top crust, use a 3- to 4-inch heart-shaped cookie cutter to cut out shapes. Arrange the pastry cutouts on top of the guava, with their sides touching and points toward the center.

Bake the tart on the middle rack of the oven for 30 to 40 minutes, or until the crust is golden brown. Let the tart cool in the pan, on a rack, for 10 minutes. If necessary, gently insert the point of a small, sharp knife between the top edge of the tart and the pan to loosen it. Carefully place the tart on top of a 1-pound can. The sides of the pan should slip down. Let the tart finish cooling on the rack. Do not remove the bottom of the pan. Just before serving, sprinkle lightly with powdered sugar. Cut into wedges or squares and serve.

SERVES 8 TO 12.

½ cup (1 stick) unsalted butter, at room temperature, plus more for the pan

2 cups sifted all-purpose flour

1 teaspoon baking powder

⅛ teaspoon salt

1 cup granulated sugar

1 large egg

1 teaspoon pure vanilla extract

1 (13- to 14-ounce) loaf guava paste, cut into ¼-inch-thick slices

1 tablespoon powdered sugar

Picante
Laurel
Nuez Moscada
Zazón Completo
Bijol
Comino Grano
Pimentón Dulce
Comino Molido

# FOUR | Cocina Nueva Onda ▣ New Wave Cooking

# Cocina Nueva Onda | New Wave Cooking

Considering how many great writers, dancers, painters, and musicians Cuba has produced, it isn't surprising that there are also some extremely talented Cuban chefs.

The frustration we most often heard expressed when talking with both home cooks and professional chefs in Cuba is the lack of available ingredients. They will say, "This recipe traditionally has ten ingredients, but since I can't get five of them, I have simplified it."

Unlike some Caribbean islands where much of the food is imported because there is not enough arable land to feed the population, Cuba is a large well-watered island with fertile soil. Historically, though wonderful fresh produce was always available, Cubans imported staples like rice and wheat, as well as canned goods. A lot of the agricultural land on the island was reserved for export crops, especially sugar. One good thing that has occurred in Cuban agriculture in the last decades is that small farmers are once again being allowed to grow fruits and vegetables in small cooperatives and individual garden plots and sell them at farmers markets. Since chemical fertilizers would be too expensive, these crops are usually organically grown.

Though it costs more, good cooks in Havana prefer to buy their produce and meat at farmers markets. El Bambú, the attractive vegetarian restaurant located in the National Botanical Gardens on the outskirts of the city, promotes the use of organically grown produce, and chefs at the best *paladares* (private restaurants) prepare wonderful food using locally grown ingredients.

Some of the dishes we tasted in Cuba, like the creamy avocado gazpacho garnished with slivers of peppery red radish at El Bambú, and the moist, perfectly grilled pork tenderloin with mango sauce at Paladar La Guarida, have a purity of taste and intensity of flavor that remind me of the innovative three-ingredient recipes of my friend, chef and cookbook author Rozanne Gold. While contemporary chefs worldwide are creating recipes with flavors so concentrated that they are almost essences, in Cuba a similar trend has developed, almost in a vacuum, through a combination of creativity and necessity.

In the United States, Nuevo Latino is a hot cooking trend, and two of its biggest stars are Cuban-American chefs Maricel Presilla, of Zafra and Cucharamama in Hoboken, New Jersey, and Douglas Rodriguez, of Ola and Ola Steak in Miami. Though they combine influences from different Latin American cuisines, many of their recipes reflect their Cuban heritage. Both Maricel and Douglas have been generous with their time and have shared some favorite recipes with us.

As these recipes show, both in Havana and in the United States, exciting things are happening in Cuban kitchens.

# Ensalada de Col, Piña, y Coco
## Cabbage, Pineapple, and Coconut Slaw

1 (8-ounce) container) key lime-flavored
  yogurt, or plain yogurt

½ cup mayonnaise

2 tablespoon fresh lime juice

1 teaspoon each ground turmeric and
  mild curry powder, or 2 teaspoons
  mild curry powder

Salt to taste

1 cup grated fresh coconut or dried,
  grated natural raw coconut

1 small green cabbage (for 8 cups
  shredded)

1 cup diced fresh or canned pineapple,
  drained

½ cup thinly sliced green onions (white
  and tender green parts)

1 to 2 tablespoons chopped fresh
  cilantro (optional)

This exotic coleslaw recipe is adapted from one served at El Bambú, the attractive vegetarian restaurant located in the Japanese gardens at the National Botanical Gardens, located on the outskirts of Havana.

In a large mixing bowl, combine the yogurt, mayonnaise, lime juice, and turmeric and curry powder. Season with salt, and stir in the coconut. Let the mixture sit for about 30 minutes to blend the flavors.

Meanwhile, shred the cabbage. Add the cabbage, pineapple, green onions, and cilantro, if using, to the coconut mixture and toss gently. Taste and adjust the seasonings, then serve.

SERVES 6.

# Ensalada de Pepino
## Cucumber Salad

Beatriz Llamas is a talented and creative cook and food writer. She was born in Spain, but currently lives in Havana with her husband and three children. Martin and I were introduced to Beatriz by a mutual friend and had the pleasure of being invited to her house for a delicious dinner. This recipe for cucumber salad is my interpretation of one included by Beatriz in her recent book *A Taste of Cuba.*

Thinly slice the cucumber and toss it with the vinegar, sugar, and salt; set aside. In a small bowl, mash together the cheese and oil with a fork; the mixture should remain slightly lumpy. Stir in the chives and season the dressing with salt and pepper. Line a serving platter with lettuce leaves. Arrange the cucumbers over the lettuce. Spoon the dressing over the cucumbers and sprinkle with mint.

SERVES 4 TO 6.

1 large, firm European-style (seedless) cucumber
1 to 2 tablespoons white wine vinegar
1 to 3 teaspoons sugar, or to taste
Salt to taste
4 ounces mild goat cheese
1/3 cup extra-virgin olive oil
2 tablespoons snipped fresh chives or finely chopped green onions
Freshly ground black pepper to taste
1 small head leaf lettuce
1 tablespoon minced fresh mint or parsley

# Cóctel de Camarones Tropical
## Tropical Shrimp Cocktail

1 ripe but firm Florida or 2 Hass
   avocados, pitted, peeled, and diced

½ head iceberg lettuce, torn into small
   pieces

1 pound fresh medium-sized shrimp,
   cooked, peeled, and deveined

½ cup fresh bitter orange juice, or
   ¼ cup regular orange juice and ¼ cup
   fresh lime juice

½ cup ketchup

2 tablespoons minced red onion

¼ cup olive oil

Salt and freshly ground black pepper to
   taste

2 to 3 ripe plum tomatoes, seeded and
   finely diced

1 to 3 fresh *ajis cachucha*, seeded and
   minced

3 to 4 tablespoons minced fresh cilantro

Fresh cilantro sprigs, lemon and/or lime
   slices or zest, *cachucha* peppers, and/
   or watercress

At first, Marty and I were perplexed when a young chef we were talking with in Cuba described a recipe containing an exotic-sounding ingredient called *ka-chup*. I felt a little silly when it turned out to be good old tomato ketchup. Ketchup is used in quite a few recipes in Cuba, and when combined with bitter orange juice, onion, olive oil, fresh tomatoes, *cachucha* chiles, and cilantro it makes an easy, refreshing, and distinctly Cuban cocktail sauce for shrimp. Serve this appetizer with *casabe*, yuca flat bread.

Cut the avocados into bite-size chunks and set aside. Fill the bottom of chilled individual glasses or serving bowls with lettuce and arrange the shrimp and avocado on top.

In a small mixing bowl, whisk together the bitter orange juice, ketchup, and onion. Gradually whisk in the oil. Taste, and season with salt and pepper. Stir in the tomatoes, chiles, and minced cilantro. Spoon the sauce over the shrimp and avocado. Garnish with cilantro sprigs and serve.

SERVES 6.

# Gaspacho de Aguacates El Bambú
## Avocado Gaspacho El Bambú

2 large, ripe Florida avocados, or 5 ripe
   Hass avocados

Juice of 1 lime

2 medium-sized cucumbers

1 cup chopped white or yellow onion

3 cups vegetable broth, fresh or canned

1 to 1½ teaspoons salt, or to taste

Freshly ground black pepper to taste

½ cup plain yogurt

¼ cup chopped fresh cilantro

¼ cup diced red radish

¼ cup diced red bell pepper

¼ cup thinly sliced green onion (green
   part only)

Interest in vegetarian cooking is a relatively new development in Cuba. Though fruits and vegetables thrive in the island's rich soil and temperate climate, fresh green salads are rare in traditional Cuban cooking and lush tropical fruits like guava, mango, and papaya are often poached in sugar syrups or used to make jams and sugary desserts. We had heard that some interesting vegetarian restaurants had opened in and around Havana and were fortunate to meet Madelaine Vázquez Gálvez, author of an interesting and innovative vegetarian cookbook titled *Cocina Ecológica en Cuba*. Eco-Restoránte El Bambú, the restaurant she manages at the National Botanical Gardens, located on the outskirts of Havana, has become a culinary destination for both Cubans and visitors from abroad. The kitchen, including the oven, is powered by solar energy, and the lighting in the restaurant is entirely natural. The menu features soups, entrées, and numerous salads and light desserts made from fresh, locally grown ingredients. This refreshing avocado-based cold soup is adapted from Madelaine's version that we enjoyed at El Bambú.

Peel, pit, and dice the avocados and toss them with the lime juice. Peel, seed, and dice the cucumbers, reserving ¼ cup for garnish. Place the avocado, cucumbers, onion, and broth in a blender or food processor. Pulse until pureed. Season the soup to taste with salt and pepper and chill until ready to serve. To serve, ladle the soup into serving bowls, top with a dollop of yogurt, and sprinkle with the reserved cucumber, the cilantro, radish, bell pepper, and green onion.

**MAKES ABOUT 6 CUPS; SERVES 4 TO 6.**

# Arroz Caribe
## Caribbean-Style Rice

2 to 3 tablespoons olive oil

¾ cup finely chopped onion

1½ teaspoons salt

¼ teaspoon freshly ground black pepper

½ teaspoon *bijol* (annatto seed seasoning)

¼ teaspoon ground cumin

1 small cinnamon (canela) stick, or ⅛ teaspoon ground cinnamon

1½ cups long-grain white rice

½ cup raisins

½ cup chopped red bell pepper

1 (13½-ounce) can unsweetened coconut milk

1 tablespoon chopped fresh cilantro or parsley

Coconut milk, herbs, and spices give this rice a creamy texture and exotic flavor. It is a delicious accompaniment for grilled pork, poultry, or fish.

Place the oil in a large saucepan over medium heat. Add the onion and sauté until translucent, 1 to 2 minutes. Stir in the salt, pepper, *bijol*, cumin, and cinnamon. Add the rice, raisins, and bell pepper and stir to coat with the oil.

Combine the coconut milk with enough hot water to make a total of 3½ cups liquid. Stir the liquid into the rice mixture and bring to a simmer, stirring, over high heat. Cover and reduce the heat to very low. Cook for 30 minutes, or until the rice is tender and most of the liquid has been absorbed. Fluff the rice with a fork, and serve sprinkled with cilantro.

SERVES 6.

# Tamales de Camaron con Pesto de Jalapeño y Queso
## Shrimp Tamales with Jalapeño and Cheese Pesto

**M**ark Miller of the Coyote Café in Santa Fe, New Mexico, calls his friend and fellow chef Douglas Rodriguez "the Mambo King of Nuevo Latino cooking." In this recipe he skillfully blends a Cuban-style fresh corn and shrimp tamale with a Mexican-inspired jalapeño and queso blanco pesto.

Make the pesto: Heat the oil in a small skillet, add the onion, garlic, and jalapeño, and sauté over medium heat for 5 minutes. Add the turmeric, stir well, and sauté for another 2 minutes.

Transfer the mixture to a food processor with steel knife blade. Add the queso blanco, and pulse until smooth. Refrigerate until ready to serve.

Make the sofrito: Heat the oil in a large skillet. Add the onion, bell peppers, and garlic and sauté over medium heat for about 15 minutes, stirring frequently. Stir in the tomato paste and remove the sofrito mixture from the heat.

Make the tamales: Rinse the fresh or dried corn husks and place them in a large pot of boiling water to cover for about 20 minutes, until soft and pliable. Place the corn kernels in a large mixing bowl and stir in the sofrito. Add the *harina fina* and cornstarch and mix well. Place small batches of the corn mixture in a food processor and pulse until pureed. Return the puree to the mixing bowl and add the sugar and salt. With a wooden spoon, fold in the shrimp.

Place a well-drained corn husk on a work surface, smoother side up. Spoon 2 tablespoons of the shrimp mixture in the middle of the husk. Fold in both long sides to enclose it. Fold up both ends to form a rectangular package about 1½ inches wide and 3 to 4 inches long. Tie the tamale securely, like a package, using kitchen string. Continue to make tamales until all of the shrimp mixture has been used.

Gently place the tamales in a large pan of boiling salted water. Reduce the heat and cook at a gentle boil until the tamales are slightly firm to the touch, about 30 minutes. Drain the tamales and let them cool slightly.

Arrange the warm tamales, still in the husks, on a serving platter. Place the chilled pesto on the side, garnish with the parsley and olives, and serve. The tamales may be frozen. Just wrap them tightly and freeze. To cook, place the frozen tamales in a pot of gently boiling water and boil for about 45 minutes.

**MAKES ABOUT 24 SMALL OR 12 LARGE TAMALES; SERVES 4 TO 6.**

### FOR THE PESTO
- 2 tablespoons extra-virgin olive oil
- 1½ tablespoons diced onion
- 1½ teaspoons minced garlic
- 1 jalapeño chile, seeded and sliced
- 1½ teaspoons ground turmeric
- 4 ounces queso blanco or Muenster cheese, cut into 1-inch chunks

### FOR THE SOFRITO
- 2 tablespoons extra-virgin olive oil
- ½ cup finely diced onion
- ½ cup finely diced red bell pepper
- ½ cup finely diced green bell pepper
- 1 tablespoon minced garlic (2 cloves)
- 1½ tablespoons tomato paste

### FOR THE TAMALES
- 4 cups fresh corn kernels (from 7 or 8 ears), husks reserved; or 1 (16-ounce) package frozen corn kernels and 1 (8-ounce) package dried corn husks
- ¼ cup *harina fina* (finely ground yellow cornmeal)
- ¼ cup cornstarch
- 1 tablespoon sugar
- 1 teaspoon salt, or to taste
- ½ pound cooked fresh shrimp, chopped
- 2 to 3 tablespoons chopped fresh parsley, preferably flat-leaf parsley
- ¼ pound whole mixed olives (such as kalamata, niçoise, and alphonso)

# Crêpes de Pollo La Guarida
## Chicken Crêpes La Guarida

**FOR THE CHICKEN FILLING**

1 pound skinless, boneless chicken
    thighs or breasts

2 tablespoons olive oil

½ cup finely chopped onion

1 clove garlic, crushed in a garlic press

2 tablespoons light rum

2 tablespoons butter

2 tablespoons flour

½ teaspoon dried herbs de Provence

¼ teaspoon salt, or to taste

½ cup light or heavy cream

½ cup chicken broth

¼ cup dry sherry

¼ teaspoon freshly grated nutmeg

Freshly ground black pepper to taste

**FOR THE MUSHROOM SAUCE**

1 ounce dried porcini mushrooms

4 tablespoons butter

2 tablespoons olive oil

1 cup finely chopped onion

4 tablespoons flour

½ cup dry sherry

½ cup chicken broth

Salt to taste

Freshly ground black pepper to taste

2 teaspoons minced fresh parsley

Spinach Crêpes (recipe follows)

La Guarida is one of Havana's most glamorous and romantic *paladares*. It gained international fame as the setting of the award-winning Cuban film *Fresas y chocolate* (*Strawberries and Chocolate*). Owners Enrique Nuñez and Odesis Baullosa work with Chef Manuel Antonio Sió Ibañez to turn out well-executed and original examples of New Cuban cooking with international flair. One of my favorite dishes from their menu is spinach crêpes filled with chicken in a nicely seasoned cream sauce, gathered like a purse and tied with a blanched scallion green. The crêpe purses are served in a pool of wild mushroom sauce and garnished with a sprinkling of piquant minced beets.

It's a spectacular presentation, but a bit hard to pull off if you are alone and cooking for several people. With that in mind, I've included a suggestion for another, more manageable presentation that tastes just as good. It may seem as though this is a dish that requires lots of preparation, but all of the components may be made in advance.

Make the chicken filling: Cut the chicken into ½-inch cubes. Place the oil in a large skillet over medium-high heat. Add the chicken and sauté until lightly browned on all sides, 6 to 8 minutes. Add the onion and garlic and cook until the onion is translucent, about 5 minutes. Remove the pan from the heat. Add the rum and carefully light it with a long kitchen match. Shake the pan gently back and forth, spooning the rum and pan juices over the chicken. When the flame subsides, add the butter, flour, herbs de Provence, and salt. Cook, stirring, for 2 minutes. Add the cream, broth, sherry, nutmeg, and pepper. Simmer for 10 minutes, then taste and adjust the seasonings. Keep warm, or if making in advance, cover and refrigerate.

Make the mushroom sauce: Place the mushrooms in a heatproof bowl and pour in 2 cups hot water. Set aside to soak for 30 minutes. Place a sieve over another bowl and line it with a coffee filter or a double thickness of cheesecloth. Swish the mushrooms around in the water to loosen any grit or sand. Remove them with a slotted spoon and set aside. Pour the mushroom soaking water through the filter into the bowl. You should have about 1½ cups liquid. Finely chop the mushrooms.

In a large skillet over medium-high heat, melt 2 tablespoons of the butter with the oil. Add the onion and sauté until slightly softened, about 2 minutes. Add the mushrooms and

*(continued)*

⅓ cup finely diced cooked beets

1 tablespoon white balsamic vinegar or
    white wine vinegar

3 tablespoons extra-virgin olive oil

Salt and freshly ground black pepper to
    taste

continue to sauté for 2 to 3 minutes. Stir in the flour and cook, stirring, for 2 minutes. Add the reserved mushroom soaking liquid, the sherry, and broth and cook, stirring, over medium heat until the sauce has thickened. Taste and season with salt and pepper. Remove from the heat, then swirl in the remaining butter and the parsley. Set aside.

Make the beet garnish: In a small bowl, combine the beets, vinegar, oil, salt, and pepper. Set aside.

Preheat the oven to 350° F. Place a crêpe with the prettiest side down on a clean work surface. Spoon 2 tablespoons of the chicken filling across the middle of the crêpe and roll it up around the filling like a tube. Continue in the same manner until all of the filling and crêpes have been used. Arrange the filled crêpes in a shallow buttered baking dish. Cover loosely with aluminum foil and bake for about 10 minutes, until heated through. To serve, spoon hot mushroom sauce over the crêpes and sprinkle the beet garnish over the tops.

SERVES 6.

# Spinach Crêpes

1 large egg

1½ cups milk

1 cup all-purpose flour

1 teaspoon salt

6 ounces fresh baby spinach leaves

½ small potato

2 to 3 tablespoons butter, melted

Place the egg, milk, flour, salt, and spinach in a blender and pulse until the batter is smooth. Place a 6-inch, well-seasoned or nonstick crêpe pan over medium heat. Dip the cut side of a potato half in the melted butter and use it to lightly grease the pan. Tilt the hot pan toward you. Ladle a scant ¼ cup of the batter into the front of the pan, then slowly tilt the pan backward to evenly coat the bottom with batter. When bubbles appear on the top, carefully turn the crêpe with a spatula and cook for 20 to 30 seconds on the other side. Remove the crêpe to a plate and repeat with the remaining batter. If you are planning to serve the crêpes immediately, stack them and cover the plate loosely with aluminum foil to keep them warm. If making the crêpes in advance, let the crêpes cool, then stack them with sheets of baking parchment or waxed paper between the crêpes. Wrap the stack in aluminum foil and refrigerate for up to 2 days or freeze for up to 1 month. When ready to use, either separate as many crêpes as you need and let them thaw or wrap still frozen crêpes individually in foil and warm them in a 300° F. oven for about 10 minutes.

MAKES 12 TO 14 CRÊPES.

# Costillitas de Puerco con Salsa de Guayaba
## Baby Back Ribs with Guava Barbecue Sauce

**C**uban-American superstar chefs like Miami's Douglas Rodriguez and New York's Alex Garcia have made guava-glazed barbecued baby back ribs a favorite new-wave Cuban dish. Though traditionally guava paste is used in pastries and tarts or served with cheese at the end of a meal, the concept of mixing sweet and savory ingredients is very Cuban. Pork, for example, is often served with sweet, caramelized fried ripe plantains or *boniato* (white sweet potato) puree.

The recipe that follows is my version of guava-glazed ribs, which are great served with hot, crisp *Palitos de Yuca Frita* (Fried Yuca Sticks; page 67).

Preheat the oven to 325° F.

Prepare the ribs: In a small bowl, combine the *Aceite de Achiote*, oregano, cumin, salt, and pepper. Rub the mixture on both sides of the ribs. Place the racks on sheets of heavy-duty aluminum foil and sprinkle the onion slices over the top. Wrap the ribs securely and place the tightly sealed packets on a baking sheet on the middle rack of the oven. Bake for 1¼ to 1½ hours, until the ribs are tender when pierced with the tip of a sharp knife.

Meanwhile, make the barbecue sauce: In a saucepan, combine the guava paste, tomato paste, molasses, vinegar, brown sugar, garlic, cumin, dry mustard, chile-garlic sauce, and sherry. Bring to a simmer over medium heat; reduce the heat to low and cook gently, stirring occasionally, until all of the ingredients are well combined.

Preheat a charcoal grill to medium-hot.

Unwrap the ribs and remove the foil, setting the onions aside. Reserving half of the sauce for dipping, brush the ribs with some of the remaining sauce and grill for 8 to 10 minutes, turning and basting frequently with more of the sauce. After turning the last time, top with the baked onions, if desired, and baste again. Serve the ribs with the reserved sauce.

**SERVES 4 TO 6.**

### FOR THE RIBS
- ¼ cup spicy or mild *Aceite de Achiote* (Achiote-Flavored Olive Oil; page 44) or olive oil
- 1 tablespoon dried Mexican oregano leaves
- 1 tablespoon ground cumin
- 1 tablespoon salt
- 1½ teaspoons freshly ground black pepper
- 4 racks baby back pork ribs
- 2 yellow onions, peeled and thinly sliced

### FOR THE BARBECUE SAUCE
- 1 (10- to 12-ounce) package guava paste, cut into small pieces
- ⅓ cup tomato paste
- ⅓ cup molasses
- ¾ cup cider vinegar or distilled white vinegar
- 3 tablespoons brown sugar
- 1 clove garlic, pressed or minced
- 4 teaspoons ground cumin
- 1 tablespoon dry mustard (Colman's)
- 3 to 4 teaspoons Asian chile-garlic sauce, or to taste
- ¾ cup dry sherry
- ¼ cup minced fresh cilantro (optional)

# Filete de Puerco a la Parrilla
## Grilled Pork Tenderloin

**2 pounds pork tenderloin**

**2 to 4 cloves garlic, peeled**

**½ teaspoon salt**

**¼ teaspoon ground cumin**

**Freshly ground black pepper to taste**

**½ cup fresh bitter orange juice, or**
 **¼ cup regular orange juice and ¼ cup**
 **fresh lime juice**

**2 to 3 tablespoons olive oil**

**1½ cups fresh *guarapo* (sugarcane juice),**
 **or 1 (11.5-ounce) can *guarapo***

**2 or 3 (8- to 10-inch) pieces sugarcane**

**Fresh cilantro and mint**

ojo, a mixture of bitter orange juice, olive oil, garlic, and spices, is the most traditional Cuban marinade. It gives the grilled pork in this recipe a piquant flavor that is complemented by a glaze of *guarapo*, juice pressed from fresh sugarcane. Serve the skewers with *Arroz Caribe* (Caribbean-Style Rice; page 142) and *Frijoles Negros* (Classic Cuban-Style Black Beans; page 47).

Partially freeze the tenderloin. With a sharp knife, cut a thin slice off the long narrow side of the tenderloin. Stand the tenderloin on this flat side and slice it into long, ribbonlike slices ¼ to ⅓ inch thick.

Crush the garlic in a garlic press and place in a small mixing bowl. With a fork, mix in the salt, cumin, and pepper to make a paste. Stir in the bitter orange juice and oil.

Place the pork in a shallow, nonreactive baking dish. Pour the marinade over the pork, turning the strips to coat with the seasonings. Let the meat marinate for at least 15 minutes.

Meanwhile, in a small saucepan over medium heat, gently boil the *guarapo*, stirring frequently, until it is reduced by half and has the consistency of a medium syrup.

Preheat a charcoal grill to medium-hot.

With a sharp chef's knife, cut the sugarcane pieces in half lengthwise, then cut each half into thirds or quarters to make skewers about ⅓ inch thick. With a sharp paring knife, pare down the skewers so that they gradually come to a sharp point at one end—like a pointed chopstick.

Thread the pork onto the sugarcane. Grill, brushing with *guarapo* syrup and turning occasionally, until the pork is cooked through and lightly caramelized, 6 to 8 minutes. Serve.

**SERVES 6.**

# Filete de Puerco con Mango La Guarida
# Pork Tenderloin with Mangoes La Guarida

This is one of my favorite recipes from Havana's most glamorous *paladar*, La Guarida. It is elegant, unusual, and quick and easy to prepare. When good mangoes are not available, I sometimes substitute ripe fresh nectarines or peeled peaches.

Halve, pit, peel, and dice 1 mango and set it aside. Reserve the other mango. In a large saucepan, heat 2 tablespoons of the oil. Add the onion, garlic, and chile and sauté over medium heat until slightly softened, 2 to 3 minutes. Stir in the cilantro, diced mango, wine, broth, and ½ tablespoon of the lime juice. Continue to cook, stirring often, over medium-low heat until the mango cooks down and the sauce smoothes out, 15 to 20 minutes.

Meanwhile, cut the tenderloin into 1½- to 2-inch-thick portions. Place the pieces cut side up between sheets of plastic wrap and flatten them with your hand to make rounds about ½ inch thick. Rub the pork lightly with 1 to 2 tablespoons of the remaining oil and season with salt and pepper.

Preheat a charcoal grill to medium-hot.

While the grill is heating, halve, pit, and peel the remaining mango. Slice the fruit into 10 to 12 slices. Drizzle the remaining lime juice and 2 to 3 teaspoons of the oil over the mango. Place the slices in a grill basket (or improvise by arranging them on a sheet of heavy-duty aluminum foil in which you have poked holes with a skewer).

Grill the pork for 3 to 5 minutes on each side, or until nicely browned and cooked through. Place the grill basket or foil on the other side of the grill grate and cook until the mango slices are hot but still hold their shape.

To finish the sauce, remove the pan from the heat and swirl in the butter, if using. Place a pool of sauce on each individual serving plate and arrange 2 or 3 pieces of pork and 2 or 3 slices of mango on top. Sprinkle with parsley and serve.

SERVES 4 TO 6.

2 large, ripe but firm mangoes

4 to 6 tablespoons olive oil

½ cup finely chopped onion

1½ teaspoons minced garlic (1 clove)

1 to 2 fresh *ajis cachucha*, or other sweet, piquant red peppers

1 tablespoon chopped fresh cilantro or parsley, plus more minced parsley for garnish

½ cup white wine

¾ cup chicken broth

1½ tablespoons fresh lime juice

1½ to 2 pounds pork tenderloin

Salt and freshly ground black pepper to taste

1 tablespoon butter (optional)

# Fricasé de Costillas de Puerco al Estilo de Chamarreta
## Braised Pork Ribs Chamarreta

4½ pounds meaty pork spare ribs, cut to order (see below)

½ cup fresh bitter orange juice, or ¼ cup regular orange juice and ¼ cup fresh lime juice

Salt to taste

4 large cloves garlic, crushed in a garlic press

8 green onions (white and tender green parts), finely chopped

Maricel Presilla is a respected food historian, restaurateur, chef, and writer. She was born in Cuba and immigrated to the United States, with her family, as a young woman. Maricel adapted this recipe from a home cook in the rural community of Chamarreta in eastern Cuba. As Maricel explains, "In this mountainous region, seasonings are Spartan, but somehow manage to do justice to the good flavor of the local pork."

This is not a classic Cuban *fricasé* as most Cubans know it, a dish made with tomatoes, bell peppers, and several other ingredients, but a pared down braise made with the few ingredients available to rural cooks. The intensity and purity of flavor obtained by limiting the number of ingredients seems so modern, however, that I decided to include this recipe in the *Cocina Nueva* chapter. Maricel suggests serving the pork with *Congrí Oriental* (Red Beans and Rice; page 59) or with boiled yuca or *boniato*.

Have your butcher separate the ribs and cut them crosswise into 2-inch sections. Rinse the ribs under cold running water and pat them dry with paper towels. Place them in a large bowl and toss with the bitter orange juice and salt; set aside for 10 minutes.

Place a large, heavy-bottomed pot or Dutch oven over medium-high heat. Working in batches, and not allowing the pieces to touch, brown the ribs in their own fat, stirring often, about 15 minutes. When the last batch of ribs are browned, return all of the ribs to the pot, add the garlic and green onions, and cook, stirring, until the vegetables are lightly browned, about 2 minutes.

Add 3 to 4 cups water (enough to halfway cover the ribs) to the pot and bring to a boil. Cover the pot tightly, lower the heat to medium, and cook until the ribs are tender, 45 minutes to 1 hour. If too much liquid remains, uncover the pot and increase the heat to medium-high. Cook until the sauce reduces and thickens to your liking. You should have enough sauce to spoon over a side of rice or tubers.

SERVES 6.

# Flan de Chocolate
## Chocolate Caramel Custard

Both in Cuba and in the United States, flan is a dessert included in the repertoires of most Cuban cooks. Sweetened condensed milk and evaporated milk are often used in flan recipes instead of fresh milk and cream, because of convenience and availability. This recipe, adapted from one created by Chef Douglas Rodriguez of Ola in Miami, is easy to make—and scrumptious. Chocolate and vanilla, both foods that originated in Meso-America, are complemented by the flavor of dark rum. For an alternative method of caramelizing the mold, see the recipe for *Flan de Leche Clásico* (Classic Flan; page 92).

**½ cup sugar**

**3 whole large eggs**

**4 large egg yolks**

**1 (14-ounce) can sweetened condensed milk**

**1 (12-ounce) can evaporated milk**

**⅓ cup dark chocolate syrup**

**1 to 2 tablespoon dark rum, or to taste**

**1 teaspoon pure vanilla extract**

Place the sugar in a heavy-bottomed saucepan over medium heat. Cook, stirring, until the sugar melts and turns a light amber color, about 10 minutes. Quickly but carefully pour the hot caramelized sugar into a 6-inch ring mold. Using oven mitts to protect your hands, turn the mold to coat the bottom and sides with caramel. Set aside while preparing the custard.

Preheat the oven to 350° F. Combine the whole eggs, yolks, sweetened condensed milk, evaporated milk, chocolate syrup, rum and vanilla in a blender or food processor. Pulse until well blended. Skim off and discard foam from on top of the custard.

Pour the custard into the caramel-coated mold. Place the mold in a larger pan and place it on the middle rack in the oven. Pour enough boiling water around the mold to come halfway up the sides. Lower the oven temperature to 325° F. Bake until the flan feels slightly firm to the touch and a toothpick inserted in the center comes out clean, 45 minutes to 1 hour.

Carefully remove the flan from the water bath and place it on a baking rack to cool. Refrigerate until chilled, at least 1 hour. When ready to serve, carefully run a thin-bladed knife around the edges of the flan to loosen it. Place a serving plate, face down, on top of the flan and, gripping the mold and the plate with both hands, invert it onto the plate. If there is caramel left in the mold, add a tablespoon or two of rum or water to the mold and swirl it over low heat until melted. Pour the caramel over the unmolded flan and serve.

SERVES 6.

# Flan de Coco La Guarida
## Coconut Flan with Curried Custard Sauce

The street outside the elegant old mansion is in disrepair. Inside, in what was once the grand entrance hall, a couple of stray dogs are camping out on dirty marble floors, and a poor family has set up housekeeping. Climbing the crumbling staircase, you may begin to have reservations about this culinary adventure, but at the second landing there is a large black door. Ring the bell and a face appears at the peephole. When you are recognized, the door swings open and you step into La Guarida, a world of well-dressed patrons and great food. The innovative menu features new Cuban recipes like this delicate coconut flan served with a subtle but exotic custard sauce.

1½ cups sugar
1 cup half-and-half
5 large eggs
1¾ cups thick fresh coconut milk, or 1 (13.5-ounce) can unsweetened coconut milk
1½ teaspoons pure vanilla extract
Curried Custard Sauce (page 154)
Guava Sauce (page 154)

Place 6 individual 6-ounce metal flan molds or ovenproof custard cups in a baking pan large enough to hold them without touching each other. Place ¾ cup of the sugar in a heavy-bottomed saucepan. Set the saucepan over medium heat and cook, stirring, until the sugar melts and the syrup takes on an amber tinge, 8 to 10 minutes. Quickly but carefully pour a portion of the caramel into each mold, immediately tilting the mold to evenly coat the bottom with caramel.

Preheat the oven to 325° F. In a heavy-bottomed saucepan, combine the half-and-half and the remaining ¾ cup sugar. Simmer, stirring, until sugar is dissolved; set aside.

In a large mixing bowl, whisk the eggs until just combined, then slowly whisk in the half-and-half mixture, coconut milk, and vanilla. Strain the custard through a fine sieve into a clean bowl, then ladle it into the caramel-coated molds. Place the baking pan on the middle rack of the oven and pour enough boiling water around the molds to come two thirds of the way up the sides of the molds. Carefully slide the rack back into the oven. Bake the flans for 50 to 60 minutes, until barely set in the middle. Remove the pan from the oven and let the custards cool slowly in the water bath. Refrigerate until ready to serve, at least 1 hour.

When ready to serve, run a thin-bladed knife around the edge of each flan, penetrating about ½ inch below the surface. Turn the molds over onto individual dessert plates. One by one, grasp the plate and the mold firmly and shake up and down until the flan drops onto the plate. Carefully remove the molds and allow the caramel to drizzle over the flans.

*(continued)*

Spoon a ribbon of Curried Custard Sauce around each flan. Place 3 or 4 dots of Guava Sauce in the custard sauce and draw the tip of a paring knife through the dots to make a decorative pattern. Serve immediately.

SERVES 6.

## Curried Custard Sauce

4 large egg yolks
½ cup sugar
1 teaspoon mild curry powder, or to taste
1¾ cups whole milk
1 teaspoon pure vanilla extract

In a mixing bowl, whisk the egg yolks until just combined. Gradually whisk in the sugar and curry powder until well combined. In a small saucepan, bring the milk to a simmer. Gradually whisk the hot milk into the egg mixture. Pour the mixture into the top of a double boiler. Pour enough boiling water into the bottom of the double boiler to come halfway up the side. (If you don't have a double boiler, improvise by putting one saucepan inside another.) Gently cook the custard, stirring slowly but constantly with a wooden spoon and reaching all over the bottom and sides. The sauce is done when it thickens enough to leave a clear track on the back of the spoon when you draw your finger across it. Stir in the vanilla. Pour the custard into a pitcher or serving bowl. Serve warm or chilled. The sauce may be made 1 to 2 days in advance and stored in the refrigerator in a covered container.

MAKES ABOUT 1½ CUPS.

## Guava Sauce

¼ cup guava jam
1 to 1½ tablespoons fresh lime juice

In a small bowl, stir the guava jam together with enough lime juice to make a pourable sauce.

MAKES ABOUT ⅓ CUP.

# Dulce de Leche con Ron
## Rum-Flavored Caramel Sauce

This version of *dulce de leche*, a popular sweet throughout Latin America, is made from two of Cuba's most famous products, sugar and rum. It's a wonderful topping for ice cream or fresh fruit and addictive enough to eat straight with a spoon. Warm the sauce and serve it over *Helado de Coco* (Coconut Ice Cream; page 158). For a tropical sundae, garnish with diced fresh pineapple and a sprinkling of toasted shredded coconut.

1 cup sugar
¼ cup light corn syrup
4 tablespoons butter
1 cup heavy cream or evaporated milk
2 to 3 teaspoons rum
½ teaspoon pure vanilla extract
Pinch of salt

Place the sugar in a 2- to 3-quart heavy-bottomed saucepan. Drizzle ½ cup water over the sugar to moisten it and stir in the corn syrup. Bring the mixture to a boil over high heat, stirring constantly. When the mixture begins to turn golden and most of the water has evaporated, after 4 to 5 minutes, quickly whisk in 2 tablespoons of the butter and continue to cook, stirring, for 2 to 3 minutes. Whisk in ¾ cup of the cream and continue to cook, stirring, until the mixture begins to thicken and turn golden brown, 4 to 5 minutes. Remove from the heat and whisk in the remaining butter and cream. Stir in the rum, vanilla, and salt and set aside to cool. Serve the sauce warm or at room temperature.

**MAKES ABOUT 1½ CUPS.**

# Flan de Calabaza Douglas Rodriguez
## Douglas Rodriguez's Pumpkin Flan

**FOR THE CARAMEL**

¾ cup sugar

**FOR THE CUSTARD**

8 large eggs

3 tablespoons sugar

¼ teaspoon ground cinnamon (optional)

¼ teaspoon freshly grated nutmeg (optional)

1½ cups cooked, pureed calabaza or pie pumpkin, or canned pumpkin puree

1 (14-ounce) can sweetened condensed milk

1 (12-ounce) can evaporated milk

**FOR THE CRUST**

½ pound gingersnaps

⅓ cup melted butter

I first became aware of the culinary wizardry of Douglas Rodriguez in 1999. At that time, Douglas was the executive chef and co-owner of Patria, one of New York City's most fashionable restaurants. Now based in Miami, he continues to produce wonderful dishes, many of which reflect his Cuban heritage. Among them is this luscious pumpkin flan with a gingersnap crust, the perfect dessert for a Thanksgiving dinner with a Cuban twist.

If cooking a fresh calabaza or pumpkin, cut it in half and remove the seeds. Cut the calabaza into pieces. Bring a pot of water to a boil, add the calabaza, and cook until tender, 20 to 30 minutes. Drain and let the calabaza cool. Peel the pieces and puree the flesh. For an alternative method of caramelizing the mold, see the recipe for *Flan de Leche Clásico* (Classic Flan; page 92).

Make the caramel: Place the sugar in a heavy-bottomed saucepan and cook, stirring, over medium heat until the sugar melts and turns a light amber color, 10 to 15 minutes. Pour the caramel into a 9-by-5-inch loaf pan and tip the pan to evenly coat the bottom. Set aside. Preheat the oven to 350° F.

Make the custard: In a large mixing bowl, using an electric mixer or whisk, beat the eggs until pale yellow. Gradually mix in the sugar, and the cinnamon and nutmeg, if using. Add the pureed calabaza, the sweetened condensed milk, and evaporated milk. Place the caramel-coated loaf pan in a larger baking pan. Pour the custard into the loaf pan. Pour enough hot water into the larger pan to come halfway up the sides of the loaf pan. Place on the middle rack of the oven and bake for 15 minutes. Lower the oven temperature to 325° F. and continue to bake until the custard is set and a knife inserted in the center comes out clean, 45 minutes to 1 hour. Remove the flan from the water bath and let it cool completely on a baking rack.

Make the crust: Place the gingersnaps in a food processor and pulse until they turn to fine crumbs. Gradually add the butter and process until well blended. Spread the crumb crust evenly over the top of the cooled flan and chill overnight in the refrigerator.

To serve, run a thin-bladed knife around the edges of the flan. Place a serving platter face down on top of the loaf pan, invert the loaf pan onto the platter, and carefully lift it off. If the flan doesn't unmold immediately, place a warm, damp towel on top of the loaf pan to warm it slightly before unmolding the flan. Slice the flan and serve.

SERVES 8 TO 10.

# Helado de Queso Crema
## Cream Cheese Ice Cream

**P**oached guava in heavy syrup is a popular dessert in Cuba. Traditionally, the fruit is accompanied by either a sharp cheese or cream cheese that complements its flavor and acts as a foil for its sweetness. When enjoying an excellent dinner at the home of cookbook author Beatriz Llamas in Havana, we were served poached guava shells with cream cheese ice cream. It was an innovative and delicious variation on the traditional theme and so memorable that I asked her permission to include it in this book. Look for canned poached guava shells in Latin American grocery stores or see Sources (page 183).

2 (8-ounce) packages cream cheese
²/₃ to 1 cup sugar, or to taste
2 tablespoons fresh lemon juice
1 teaspoon salt
1 teaspoon pure vanilla extract
2 cups heavy cream
1 cup whole milk

With an electric mixer at medium speed, beat the cream cheese together with the sugar, lemon juice, salt, and vanilla. With the mixer running, gradually add the cream and milk and continue to beat until fluffy. Transfer the mixture to an ice-cream maker and freeze according to the manufacturer's directions.

**MAKES ABOUT 1 QUART; SERVES 4 TO 6.**

# Helado de Coco
## Coconut Ice Cream

2½ cups whole milk

Peeled, diced flesh of 1 fresh coconut, or
  2½ cups packaged unsweetened
  shredded coconut

6 large egg yolks

⅔ cup sugar

⅛ teaspoon salt

2 cups heavy cream

½ teaspoon pure vanilla extract

At El Buganvil, a popular *paladar* located on the outskirts of Havana, we enjoyed an excellent coconut ice cream attractively served in coconut shells. Coconut is a popular ingredient in Cuban desserts and sweets. That very morning at a farmers market, we had watched a vendor crack coconut shells and use a crank-style grater to shred the fresh coconut flesh. Some coconut confections are just too sweet for me, but this ice cream is delicate and refreshing enough to be topped with another Cuban specialty, the luscious *Dulce de Leche con Ron* (Rum-Flavored Caramel Sauce; page 155).

If you are able to find a fresh coconut, but don't have a coconut grater, first crack the nut by hitting it in the middle with the back of a heavy cleaver. When the shell has cracked, insert the thin edge of the blade and pry it open. Save the sweet liquid inside to drink. Place the halves of the coconut in a 300° F. oven for 15 to 20 minutes, until the flesh starts to separate from the shell. Using the point of a paring knife, carefully lift out the flesh in chunks and peel off and discard the thin layer of dark brown skin with a vegetable peeler. Cut the white flesh into chunks. If fresh coconuts aren't available, substitute packaged shredded coconut. If using sweetened shredded coconut, reduce the amount of sugar in the recipe to ½ cup.

In a medium saucepan, bring the milk to a simmer over medium heat. Place the coconut in a blender, or a food processor with a steel knife blade, and add half of the hot milk. With the lid firmly in place, pulse until the coconut is finely chopped. Pour the mixture into a fine sieve placed over a bowl. Using a wooden spoon or spatula, press as much liquid out of the coconut as possible and collect it in the bowl below. Return the coconut to the blender, add the remaining milk, and repeat the procedure. You should end up with about 2 cups coconut-flavored milk.

In the top of a double boiler, whisk the egg yolks, sugar, and salt for 3 to 4 minutes, or until pale yellow. Gradually whisk in the milk mixture. Place the top of the double boiler over a pan of simmering water and cook, stirring constantly, for about 10 minutes, or until the custard thickens enough to coat the back of the spoon. Remove the top pan from over the water and stir in the cream and vanilla. Chill the mixture for 30 minutes, then pour into an ice-cream maker and freeze according to the manufacturer's directions.

**MAKES ABOUT 1 QUART; SERVES 4 TO 6.**

# Pastel de Coco y Calabaza
## Coconut and Pumpkin Tart

**FOR THE CRUST**

¾ cup (1½ sticks) good-quality unsalted
   butter

1½ tablespoons almond oil or mild
   cooking oil

2 tablespoons sugar

½ teaspoon salt

¼ cup finely chopped crystallized ginger

2 to 2⅓ cups all-purpose flour

**FOR THE FILLING**

¾ cup sugar

1 tablespoon cornstarch

1 teaspoon ground cinnamon

½ teaspoon ground ginger

½ teaspoon salt

¼ teaspoon ground cloves

3 large eggs

2 cups cooked, pureed calabaza or pie
   pumpkin, or 1 (15-ounce) can pumpkin
   puree

1 (13.5-ounce) can unsweetened coconut
   milk

Whipped cream

Shredded toasted coconut

Calabaza (West Indian pumpkin) is an orange-fleshed squash with an orange, green, or striped skin. The best—and most widely available—substitutes for calabaza in the United States are New England sweet pie pumpkins and butternut or acorn squash.

This is one of the best pumpkin desserts I've ever tasted. The crust is crisp, tender, and flavorful, and the addition of coconut milk makes the filling light, creamy, and delicate.

Make the crust: Preheat the oven to 400° F. In a large microwave-safe mixing bowl, combine the butter, oil, ⅓ cup water, the sugar, and salt. Microwave at high power until the butter is melted and the mixture is boiling. Stir in the crystallized ginger. Using a fork, gradually stir in the flour, stirring just until the dough reaches a soft but workable consistency. Pat the dough evenly into the bottom and up the sides of a 9- to 10-inch springform cake pan. Prick the bottom in a few places with the fork. Gently press a sheet of baking parchment or aluminum foil into the shell and fill it with dried beans or pie weights. Bake the crust for 10 minutes. Carefully lift out the parchment and beans. If the bottom crust has puffed up, prick it with a fork and gently press it down. Return the crust to the oven for an additional 10 minutes, or until it just begins to firm up and turn golden. Set aside until ready to fill; leave the oven on.

Make the filling: While the crust is baking, in a small bowl combine the sugar, cornstarch, cinnamon, ginger, salt, and cloves. In a large bowl, using an electric mixer, beat the eggs until pale yellow. Gradually beat in the sugar mixture and the pureed calabaza.

Meanwhile, in a large, heavy-bottomed saucepan over medium-low heat, bring the coconut milk just to a simmer. With the mixer running, gradually add the hot coconut milk to the calabaza mixture. Pour the calabaza mixture into the saucepan and cook gently, stirring constantly, over medium-low to low heat until the mixture thickens to the consistency of a pourable custard, 8 to 10 minutes.

Pour the custard into the partially baked crust. Lower the oven temperature to 350° F. Bake the tart on the middle rack of the oven for 40 to 50 minutes, until the filling is set and slightly firm to the touch. Let the tart cool in the pan for about 10 minutes, then carefully remove the rim. Place the tart on a rack and let it cool completely. Don't attempt to remove the bottom of the pan before serving, as you may break the crust. Decorate the top of the pie with swirls of whipped cream and a sprinkling of toasted coconut.

SERVES 8 TO 10.

# Plátanos a la Tentacíon con Ron
## Temptation Plantains Flamed with Rum

This elegant dessert is as easy to make as it is spectacular. It is a variation on the classic baked ripe plantains that are served in Cuba as a side dish. Serve the plantains as they are, or spoon them over *Helado de Coco* (Coconut Ice Cream; page 158).

Peel the plantains and cut them in half crosswise, then lengthwise, then cut in half again lengthwise. Each plantain should be in 8 pieces. Sprinkle the plantains with the lime juice and set aside.

In a chafing dish or large skillet over medium heat, melt the butter. Add the plantains and sauté for 2 to 4 minutes, until golden. Sprinkle with the brown sugar and cinnamon and gently turn the plantain pieces, over medium-low heat, until well coated. Remove from the heat. Pour in the rum. Carefully ignite the rum with a long match. Gently shake the chafing dish back and forth. When the flames subside, sprinkle the plantains with the nutmeg, if using. Serve immediately.

SERVES 6.

**3 medium-size ripe plantains**

**1½ tablespoons fresh lime juice**

**6 tablespoons butter**

**6 tablespoons brown sugar**

**¼ teaspoon ground cinnamon**

**⅛ teaspoon freshly grated nutmeg (optional)**

**⅓ cup *añejo* (aged) rum or light rum**

# FIVE | Bebidas ▣ Beverages

# Bebidas | Beverages

Some Cuban beverages, like café Cubano, are well known, and rum-based cocktails like mojitos, daiquiris, and Cuba Libres have become international favorites, but others, like *bul*, a strange-sounding but very refreshing beer cooler, and *saoco*, a simple but luscious concoction made with coconut milk and rum, were new discoveries for us.

Cuba's most important beverages are coffee, rum, fruit drinks, chocolate, and, surprisingly, beer. Wine is imported, and priced beyond the means of most Cubans as an everyday beverage, though sangria may be served on special occasions. Beer is expensive but popular in Cuba. There are several breweries on the island, but the best domestic Cuban beer is Cristal, a historic brand that was originally brewed by La Tropical, a brewery founded in Havana in 1888 by the Blanco Herrera family.

Coffee is a symbol of Cuban hospitality. Visit a Cuban at home or at his or her place of business and you will be offered a *cafecito*, a thimble-sized cup of strong, sweet coffee. First introduced to the island in 1748 by José Antonío Gelabert, who planted a few Arabica coffee seedlings he brought from Haiti, coffee was truly established fifty years later, when Frenchmen fleeing the Haitian revolution established thriving coffee plantations in the rich, loamy soil of the Nipe and Sagua-Baracoa mountains.

Rum is produced throughout the Caribbean, and each island's rum has its own distinctive character. *Aguardiente,* a rough home-brewed version, has been made in Cuba since the seventeenth century, but it was not until the mid-nineteenth century that Don Facundo Bacardi y Maso, a Spanish immigrant from Catalonia, first produced high-quality rum on the island and established the award-winning brand that became so famous. Cuba remains known for its light-bodied, crisp, white or "light" rum—the perfect rum to use in rum-based fruit drinks like daiquiris and mojitos.

The first cacao seedlings were brought to Cuba from Central America by the Spanish in the sixteenth century. Fashionable among the Spanish upper classes, Cubans also loved chocolate, and it remained the breakfast beverage of choice for prosperous Cubans until the nineteenth century, when coffee drinking became the rage in Havana.

Cuban beverages reflect the diversity of cultural influences on the island. Drinks like coffee, brought from Africa by way of Europe and Haiti, chocolate, from MesoAmerica, beer, from Europe, and rum, made from sugarcane, a grass that originated in the islands around Indonesia, have all flourished and taken on a uniquely Cuban identity.

# Batido de Mamey
## Mamey Shake

1 cup unsweetened mamey colorado
  puree, fresh or frozen

2 cups cold milk

2 tablespoons honey or sugar, or to
  taste

1 cup cracked ice

Big breakfasts are not the custom in Cuba, but Cuban families often start out the morning with a nourishing fresh fruit *batido*. Though she lives in Colorado, Cuban-American cook Barbara Trujillo likes to make breakfast *batidos* for her four children. Mamey colorado (red mamey sapote), a large, sweet tropical fruit with beautiful orange pulp, is very popular in Cuba and south Florida. It is too fragile to be widely distributed outside of Florida, but several sources in the Miami area ship the frozen puree to customers all over the United States. Barbara is lucky: Her in-laws in Florida keep her freezer in Colorado well stocked with mamey from their backyard!

Of course, *batidos* are made with many different fruits; if you can't get mamey, substitute other tropical fruits, like papayas, mangoes, or bananas, that are more widely available in supermarket produce departments. The proportions may change a bit, depending upon the sweetness and density of the fruit, but the recipe is basically the same. For a special treat, try substituting vanilla ice cream or frozen yogurt for the ice.

Place the mamey, milk, honey, and ice in a blender. Pulse until smooth and frothy. Serve in tall frosted glasses.

**SERVES 4.**

## Batido de Plátano y Ron | Banana and Rum Shake

1 small banana

½ cup vanilla ice cream

½ cup cold milk

2 ounces *añejo* (aged rum) or light rum

Freshly grated nutmeg (optional)

This is a *batido* for grown-ups. Rum and fruit is a great combination, but add a little ice cream and it's dynamite. Be careful with this one, as it goes down easy but packs a wallop! For those who don't imbibe, it is also good without the rum.

Place the banana, ice cream, milk, and rum in a blender. Pulse until smooth and frothy. Pour into chilled tall glasses. Sprinkle with nutmeg and serve.

**SERVES 2.**

# Durofrios de Mango
## Mango Fruitsicles

2 ripe, medium-size mangoes, or 2 cups
    frozen mango pulp
³/₄ cup sugar
³/₄ cup cracked ice, or 6 ice cubes

*D*urofrios in several different tropical fruit flavors, are a popular treat for children in Cuba. They may be made at home using ice trays, if the family has a refrigerator/freezer, or you can buy them from the ice cream man who makes the rounds on his bicycle-powered cart.

My friend Barbara Trujillo remembers eating *durofrios* when she was growing up in a Cuban-American neighborhood in New Jersey. Since fresh mangoes are available at most supermarkets in the United States, Barbara, who now lives in Colorado, often makes these easy, fresh tropical fruitsicles for her four children.

If using fresh mangoes, place a mango on its side on a cutting board. With a sharp knife, cut straight down on either side of the large, flat-sided pit in the middle of the mango. Scoop out the mango pulp from both sides. Repeat with the second mango. Place the mango pulp, sugar, ¹/₂ cup water, and the ice in a blender or a food processor with steel knife blade. Blend until smooth and frosty. Pour the mixture into Popsicle molds or ice trays and freeze until solid, about 2 hours.

**MAKES 6 *DUROFRIOS*.**

# Cubanito
## Cuban Bloody Mary

We first tasted this Cuban version of the Bloody Mary while seated on the veranda of the atmospheric old Hotel Presidente in Havana. It gives a traditional favorite a tropical twist.

Place all the ingredients except the garnishes in a chilled tall glass and stir. Garnish with the celery stick, lime wedge, and cilantro and serve.

SERVES 1.

½ cup cracked ice
2 teaspoons fresh lime juice
½ to ¾ teaspoon sugar, or to taste
⅛ teaspoon salt
1 teaspoon Worcestershire sauce
Dash of hot sauce
1½ ounces light rum
3 ounces tomato juice
Garnishes: 1 celery stick, 1 lime wedge, and 1 fresh cilantro sprig

# Bul | Beer Cooler

Palma Cristal, with its distinctive green label and palm tree logo, is the most popular beer in Cuba. It is a light, refreshing, medium-dry Pilsner-style beer, the perfect compliment to Cuban food. At hotels and tourist restaurants, a bottle of Cristal costs the convertible peso equivalent of about three dollars U.S.

Place the beer, lime juice, sugar, and ice in a blender and pulse until frothy. Serve in chilled tall glasses garnished with the lime slices.

SERVES 2.

1 (12-ounce) bottle beer
Juice of 2 limes (about ½ cup)
¼ cup sugar
1 cup crushed ice
Lime slices

# Chocolate Frío
## Cold Chocolate

1 (1-ounce) square pure dark
  unsweetened chocolate (see Sources,
  page 183) or baking chocolate
1 cup milk
2 to 3 teaspoons honey, or to taste

**O**n our first day in Havana, Marty and I visited friends who had cacao trees growing in their garden. This encouraged me to learn more about the history of chocolate in Cuba, and the chocolate museum at La Casa de La Cruz Verde, a Spanish colonial house in old Havana became one of my favorite places in Cuba. The museum is the source of both recipes offered here. First introduced by the Spanish from Mexico and Central America in the sixteenth century, cacao trees thrived in Cuba. Chocolate connoisseurs praise the powerful flavor and smoky undertones of Cuban chocolate.

In a heavy-bottomed saucepan over low heat, melt the chocolate with the honey to make a paste. Whisk in the milk. Place the mixture in the freezer until well chilled. Put it in a blender and blend until frothy. Pour into a chilled tall glass and serve.

SERVES 1.

## Chocolate Azteca | Aztec Hot Chocolate

1 (1-ounce) square pure unsweetened
  dark chocolate (see Sources, page
  183)
⅛ teaspoon freshly grated nutmeg
⅛ teaspoon ground cinnamon
Pinch of freshly ground black pepper or
  ground hot chile
1½ cups milk
1 teaspoon cornstarch, dissolved in
  ¼ cup cold water
¼ teaspoon pure vanilla extract
Sugar to taste

**T**he purpose of La Casa de La Cruz Verde is to acquaint visitors with the history of chocolate and to allow them to indulge in Cuban-grown and -processed chocolate in the form of beverages and hand-dipped bonbons. Joining the rest of the chocoholics, Marty and I sat at small marble tables and sipped slightly spicy "Aztec" hot chocolate, and frosty and refreshing cold chocolate. The Aztecs of central Mexico added spices to their chocolate and drank it unsweetened, and this is the museum's version of that ancient beverage. Sugar is served separately for those of us who like it sweet.

In a small, heavy-bottomed saucepan over low heat, melt the chocolate with the nutmeg, cinnamon, and pepper. Whisk in the milk, cornstarch mixture, and vanilla. Cook over medium heat, whisking constantly, until the chocolate is hot, frothy, and thickened. Pour into cups and sweeten to taste with sugar.

SERVES 2.

# Café Cubano
## Cuban Coffee

**3 cups water**

**3 to 5 tablespoons dark-roasted, finely ground coffee, or to taste**

**8 teaspoons sugar, or to taste**

Cubans like their coffee strong, hot, and sweet, and have very definite ideas about how to brew it. The coffee itself is dark roasted and more finely ground than Italian espresso. You may grind it yourself using dark-roasted beans, preferably arabica beans, or buy one of the brands of Cuban-style ground coffees, such as Bustello, Pilón, El Pico, or La Llave, sold in the international coffee section of grocery stores in the United States.

Here are three ways to brew the perfect cup of Cuban coffee: the traditional method and the now more common methods using a stovetop espresso pot or electric espresso machine.

Small demitasse cups of sweet black coffee are consumed throughout the day and particularly at the end of a meal. Those who don't like it as strong ask for a *cortadito*, a small cup with a little hot milk added. For breakfast, Cuban adults and children often drink *café con leche,* in a large cup. The general proportions are 1/2 to 3/4 cup hot milk to 1/4 cup hot coffee.

The traditional brewing method: In a saucepan over medium-high heat, bring 3 cups water to a boil. Add the coffee and boil for 2 to 3 minutes. Place the sugar in a coffee serving pot. Set a cotton straining cone (sold in Cuban grocery stores) in the top of the pot. Pour the coffee mixture into the cone and let it drip into the pot. After the first 2 to 3 teaspoons of coffee are brewed, stir the coffee and sugar together to make a smooth paste. Let the remaining coffee drip into the pot and stir until sugar is completely dissolved. Serve in demitasse cups.

The espresso pot method: Fill the bottom half of a two-part Moka coffeepot to the "MAX" line with cold water. Fill the top half loosely with coffee. Place the pot over medium heat. Put the sugar in a separate coffee serving pot, or a large heatproof glass measuring cup. When the coffee begins to bubble up into the top of the pot, add the first 2 to 3 teaspoons of brewed coffee to the sugar and stir to make a paste. When the remaining coffee rises to the top of the pot, pour it into the serving pot and stir until the sugar is dissolved. Serve in demitasse cups.

The espresso machine method: Follow the instructions for your machine, but add sugar to the pitcher the coffee drips into and stir it together with the first 2 to 3 teaspoons of brewed coffee. Fill with the remaining coffee and stir until the sugar dissolves. Serve in demitasse cups.

SERVES 6.

# Cuba Libre
## Free Cuba (Rum and Coca-Cola)

At the end of the Spanish-American War in 1898, Cuban patriots and U.S. Marines celebrated their victory over the Spanish by mixing together Cuba's famous rum and a new American beverage, Coca-Cola, that had been invented in 1886 by Dr. John Pemberton, a pharmacist from Atlanta, Georgia. To cut the sweetness, someone added a squeeze of lime and a chunk of ice. The drink was an instant hit and remains so to this day. Cuba Libres are strong, but the originals were even more potent because until 1905 the formula for Coca-Cola contained cocaine as well as the caffeine-rich kola nut.

**1½ ounces light rum**

**4 ice cubes**

**2 tablespoons fresh lime juice**

**6 ounces ice-cold Coca-Cola**

**Lime twist**

Place the rum and ice in a tall glass. Add the lime juice, pour in the Coca-Cola, and stir. Garnish with the lime twist and serve.

SERVES 1.

# Daiquiri El Floridita
## Daiquiri from El Floridita Bar

The invention of the daiquiri is attributed to Jennings Cox, an American mining engineer who was stationed at the Daiquiri Iron Mines, near Santiago de Cuba, in the late 1890s. It was at El Floridita, in Havana, however, that this refreshing but potent drink first won international acclaim.

❖❖ ❖❖ ❖❖

To make this drink the traditional way, put the rum, lime juice, sugar, and ice in a cocktail shaker and shake until frothy. Another, more contemporary option is to put all the ingredients except the mint in a blender and blend on high speed until smooth and frothy. Serve in a chilled cocktail glass and garnish with mint.

SERVES 1.

**2 ounces light rum**
**2 tablespoons fresh lime juice**
**1 to 3 teaspoons sugar, or to taste**
**1/2 cup cracked ice**
**Fresh mint sprig**

## Daiquiri Ernest Hemingway | Ernest Hemingway's Daiquiri

Among El Floridita's most famous patrons was Ernest Hemingway, who considered it one of his favorite hangouts. Even after all these years, it is impossible to enter El Floridita without remembering Papa Hemingway. His favorite stool at one end of the bar is chained off so no one else can sit there, and a life-size bust of the author presides over the room. This variation on the classic daiquiri, made without sugar, was supposedly invented by Hemingway because he was diabetic.

❖❖ ❖❖ ❖❖

In a blender, blend all the ingredients except the mint at high speed until thick. Serve in a chilled martini glass, garnished with a slice of lime.

SERVES 1.

**6 tablespoons fresh grapefruit juice**
**2 ounces white rum**
**1 teaspoon maraschino liqueur or maraschino cherry juice**
**1 teaspoon fresh lime juice**
**1/2 cup crushed ice**
**Slice of lime**

# Mojito Criollo
## Creole-Style Mojito

6 fresh mint leaves

¼ teaspoon finely grated lime zest

2 tablespoons fresh lime juice

¼ cup *guarapo* (sugarcane juice) or
sugar syrup

2 ounces light rum

½ cup cracked ice

¼ cup 7-Up or soda water

1 stick sugarcane

1½ teaspoons sugar

Juice of ½ lime

2 fresh mint sprigs

1½ ounces white rum

2 ice cubes

Soda water

The mojito is a drink that originated on sugar plantations in Cuba. Cane cutters working in the fields were provided by the plantation owner with barrels of *guarapo*, fresh sugarcane juice. The workers often added a bunch of fresh mint, *hierba buena*, to the *guarapo* to flavor it, and on special occasions they spiked it with *aguardiente*, a rough form of rum. Over the years, the drink became fashionable and evolved.

The recipe that follows is an updated version of the original. It calls for *guarapo*, which is sold fresh in Miami and other Cuban enclaves in the United States and is also available in cans in many Latin American grocery stores. If you can't find *guarapo*, combine 2 tablespoons sugar and ¼ cup water in a small saucepan and stir over medium heat until the sugar is dissolved and the syrup turns clear. Chill the syrup before using.

In a mortar, crush the mint together with the lime zest. Combine the mint, zest, lime juice, *guarapo*, rum, and ice in a cocktail shaker. Shake well to release the mint aroma. Pour into a tall, narrow glass and top with 7-Up. Garnish with the sugarcane stick.

SERVES 1.

## Mojito La Bodeguita del Medio | Mojito from La Bodeguita del Medio

Though it has turned into a bit of a tourist trap, La Bodeguita del Medio is worth at least one visit. It was here that Ernest Hemingway stopped in each day he was in Havana to drink a mojito. This is the famous bar's official recipe.

Put the sugar and lime juice in a highball glass. Add one mint sprig and use the back of a stirring spoon to crush it into the sugar and lime juice. Add the rum and ice. Fill the glass with soda water. Stir and serve, garnished with the remaining sprig of mint.

SERVES 1.

# Ponche de Leche Cubano
## Hot Rum Punch

T he next time you have a cold or can't sleep, consider trying this soothing hot punch. It is the perfect nightcap!

In a heatproof mixing bowl, whisk together the egg yolks and sugar until pale yellow. Gradually whisk in the hot milk. Pour the mixture into a heavy-bottomed saucepan or the top of a double boiler over simmering water. Cook, stirring with a wooden spoon, over medium-low heat until the custard thickens enough to coat the back of the spoon. Stir in the rum and pour the *ponche* into cups or mugs. Sprinkle with nutmeg and serve.

SERVES 2.

**3 large egg yolks**
**3 tablespoons sugar**
**2 cups hot milk**
**2 ounces *añejo* (aged rum)**
**Freshly grated nutmeg**

# Saoco
## Rum and Coconut Drink

½ cup fresh or canned unsweetened
　coconut milk
1½ ounces light rum
1 tablespoon sugar
¼ teaspoon fresh lime juice
¾ cup cracked ice

Varadero is one of the most famous of Cuba's many beautiful beaches. With its white sand shaded by coconut palms, it is the perfect place to stretch out in a lounge chair, look out at an azure sea, and sip a frosty *saoco* served in a coconut shell. The origin of this exotic drink can be traced back to the old Cuban custom of opening a green coconut and adding a shot of *aguardiente*, sugarcane white lightning, to the coconut water for an instant cocktail. A favorite treat at the beach (shown at right) is to split open a coconut and pour coffee in to mix with the coconut milk—and a shot of rum.

Combine all the ingredients in a blender and blend until frothy. Serve in a coconut shell or a tall chilled glass.

SERVES 1.

# Glossary of Cuban Ingredients and Cooking Terms

**Achiote, annatto:** The small, hard, brick-red seeds of *Bixa orellana*, a tropical tree. Sold in Cuba either in the form of seeds or in a powdered spice seasoning called *bijol*. The flavor of achiote is subtle; its main use in cooking is to impart a beautiful red or golden color to other foods. It is sometimes substituted for the much more expensive saffron.

**Aguacate (avocado):** Cuban avocados, like those grown in Florida, are large and buttery in texture. Smaller California avocados may be substituted.

**Aguardiente:** A powerful, often home-brewed liquor made from sugarcane juice.

**Ajiaco:** Cuba's national dish, a stew or thick soup made with tubers, vegetables, and meats that can be traced back to the island's original Native American inhabitants.

**Aji cachucha, aji dulce, or rocotillo:** Small red, yellow, or green pattypan squash-shaped chiles. They look a lot like habaneros, but are mild to moderately hot in flavor. If they are not available, substitute sweet bell peppers or a medium-hot chile such as Anaheim.

**Aji picante (hot chile):** Any small, home-grown hot chile such as *chile de arbol*, bird pepper, or pequin. They are often steeped in vinegar, rum, or sherry to make a hot sauce.

**Almendras (almonds):** Almonds were brought to Cuba from Spain and are used in many Cuban dishes.

**Anón:** See *Guanábana*.

**Azafrán (saffron):** An expensive spice made from the stigma of a variety of crocus grown in Spain. Saffron is used to add color, flavor, and aroma to many Cuban dishes.

**Bacalao (salt cod):** Salt-preserved dried fish often used in Cuban recipes.

**Bijol:** Condiment used to give rice a yellow color, containing ground annatto seeds, corn flour, and ground cumin. It is often substituted for the more expensive saffron.

**Bitter orange:** *See* Naranja agria.

**Boniato (Cuban white sweet potato):** Often sold in Florida as Florida yam, it has thick, brown skin and white, mealy flesh and tastes like a combination of the white potato and the American sweet potato. It can be boiled, fried, pureed, or made into *boniatillo*, a sweet dessert.

**Calabaza (West Indian pumpkin):** A large, round squash with firm, orange flesh and a sweet flavor, it is added to soups and stews, boiled and served as a vegetable with garlic sauce, or made into a custard. It is sold in precut chunks at Hispanic markets. Sweet pie pumpkins and butternut and Hubbard squash are good substitutes.

**Casabe:** An unleavened yuca (cassava) bread, a traditional staple for Cuba's early Native American inhabitants. It is sold at Cuban grocery stores.

**Cherimoya:** A tropical fruit with an artichoke-like shape and creamy flesh with a flavor somewhere between pineapple and banana.

Cherimoya is used to make ice cream, sorbet, and smoothies. See also *Guanábana*.

**Chorizo:** A dry-cured Spanish sausage highly seasoned with garlic and paprika. Unlike fresh Mexican-style chorizo, the Spanish-Cuban variety is ready to eat. In Cuba, chorizo is frequently used in stews and paellas. It comes in several different sizes from two to eight inches in length. Though usually sold wrapped in plastic wrap, they are also sometimes packed in lard.

**Cilantro, Chinese parsley, or fresh coriander:** An herb with roundish, lobed leaves similar in appearance to flat-leaf parsley. Cilantro has a bold sagelike flavor with citrus overtones. In Cuba, it is used interchangeably with a similar-tasting herb, *culantro*.

**Coco (coconut):** Fruit of the coconut palm. When ripe, it is green and shiny on the outside, and filled with a clear liquid that is good to drink. The flesh is white and tender and can be scooped out with a spoon. It is used in a variety of dessert recipes. When dried, as they are usually sold in grocery stores, coconuts have a hard, brown shell. There is less liquid inside, though it is still good to drink. The shredded fresh or dried meat is used as is, or steeped in boiling water or milk and strained to make coconut "milk" and "cream."

**Comino (cumin):** Cumin seed is the dried fruit of a Mediterranean plant of the parsley family (*apiaceae unbelliferae*). It is used either whole or ground in Cuban cooking.

**Culantro:** A dark green flat-leaf herb with a distinctive sawtooth edge, *culantro* tastes like strong cilantro, with a slightly bitter aftertaste. It is used interchangeably with cilantro.

**Empanada:** Baked or deep-fried pastry turnover, filled with chicken, meat, fish, or other fillings.

**Falda (beef brisket):** The cut of beef most often used to make classic Cuban dishes like *ropa vieja* and *vaca frita*.

**Frijoles colorados (dried red beans):** A Cuban staple, often combined with white rice to make *congrí*, a speciality of Cuba's eastern provinces.

**Frijoles negros (dried black beans):** A Cuban staple, often combined with white rice to make *Moros y Christianos*.

**Fruta bomba (papaya):** The papaya most often found in Cuba is the large Mexican variety with a red-orange flesh. When ripe, the skin turns yellow and the fruit is soft to the touch. Papaya is thought to aid digestion and act as a natural diuretic. Some people have a sensitivity to an enzyme that the fruit secretes, so it is advisable to wear rubber gloves when peeling and cutting up papayas, and to wash your hands thoroughly after handling them.

**Guanábana, soursop, or anòn:** A large green fruit native to tropical North and South America. It belongs to the *Annonaceae* family, which includes custard apple and cherimoya. If hard, store the fruit at room temperature until it gives a little when squeezed. The pulp is creamy in color and texture. It is often used to make sorbets, ice creams, and fruit smoothies. Neither the skin nor the large black seeds are edible. The frozen pulp is sold in some Latin American grocery stores.

**Guarapo (fresh sugarcane juice):** A popular drink in Cuba, *guarapo* is usually served over ice with a squeeze of lime. It is pressed and sold fresh at some Latin American markets in the United States, and is also usually available in the soda section in cans.

**Guayaba (guava):** A green, oval fruit with sweet red, pink, or white flesh and small edible seeds. When ripe, it is soft to the touch. It is eaten out of hand, poached in sugar syrup, used for jellies, preserves, and marmalade, and also made into *membrillo*, a hardened paste that is sold in thirteen-, sixteen-, and eighteen-ounce loaves. Guava paste is used in desserts or served with crackers and Cuban *queso blanco* (similar to farmer's cheese) or cream cheese.

**Harina de maiz:** In Cuba, *harina* (flour) usually means finely ground yellow cornmeal. Cornmeal is boiled and eaten as a porridge or baked or mixed with meat to make *tamal en cazuela*, tamale in a casserole. When it is unavailable, regular ground cornmeal may be substituted. It is important to start cornmeal cooking in cold water, not boiling water. It should then be brought to a boil, and whisked frequently to prevent sticking.

**Jamón de cocinar (cooking ham):** The ham most often used in Cuban recipes is called *jamón de cocinar*. It is sold in chunks at Hispanic markets. Regular ham steak may be substituted.

**Limón (lime):** Both green Persian limes and *limónes criollos*, Key limes, are used in Cuban cooking. Lime juice is used for marinating meat, fish, and poultry, and as a flavoring in many Cuban recipes.

**Malanga (taro root):** Two different varieties of taro are used in Cuban cooking: *Malanga blanca*, also known as *guaguí*, has white flesh and brown skin. The flesh turns slightly gray when boiled, and the flavor resembles that of the white potato. It may be boiled, deep-fried, or added to soups. *Malanga amarilla* is a yellow-fleshed variety. It has a yellow interior and a stronger flavor than its white sister. The flesh is tough and must be eaten as soon as it is cooked or it will harden. All varieties of *malanga* must be peeled and cooked before eating.

**Mamey colorado (red mamey sapote):** A favorite fruit in Cuba for making smoothies, mameys are about the size of a large sweet potato. Their thin skin is rough and brown and resembles sandpaper, but the beautiful salmon-colored flesh is smooth and creamy and has a sweet, delicate, berrylike flavor. The fruit ripens best at room temperature. When ripe, it gives when gently squeezed.

**Mango:** A yellow, orange, or red fruit with a large pit, thin skin, and a sweet, peachlike flavor. Mangoes ripen best in a closed brown paper bag at room temperature. When ripe, they have brown spots and are soft to the touch. Mangoes secrete a fluid that can cause an allergic reaction in some people, so it is a good idea to wear rubber gloves when peeling and cutting up the fruit, and wash your hands after touching them. They are used in drinks, ice cream, sorbet, salads, mousses, marmalade, and other dishes.

**Mojo:** A sauce made with bitter orange juice, garlic, salt, and sometimes olive oil. It is used as a sauce for cooked yuca and other vegetables. It is also used as a marinade for fish, meat, and poultry. Bottled *mojo* sauce is sold at Latin American grocery stores, but freshly made *mojo* is best.

**Ñame (tropical yam):** A large brown-black, thick-skinned tuber with white or yellow flesh. The flesh has a bland flavor and may be boiled, fried, sautéed, or pureed. Chunks of boiled *ñame* are used in *ajiaco criollo* (Cuban creole stew). After peeling, it may be stored in the refrigerator for two to three days in acidulated water before cooking. *Ñame* does not freeze well.

**Naranja agria (bitter orange):** The Seville orange, a bitter citrus fruit whose juice is used in marinades, and juice and peel are used to make marmalade. When bitter orange juice is not available, substitute half regular orange juice mixed with half fresh lime juice. Seville oranges are available at Hispanic markets.

**Oregano:** An aromatic herb related to mint. The Mexican variety is stronger in flavor than Mediterranean oregano. Most Cuban recipes call for crumbled dried oregano leaves.

**Picadillo:** Ground meat sautéed with a sofrito of vegetables, spices, and raisins. Picadillo is served with rice as a main course, and also may be used as a filling for vegetables or empanadas.

**Pimentón (paprika):** Finely ground sweet or hot dried red chiles. Most Cuban cooks prefer mild Spanish paprika. It is used to flavor sauces and chicken and meat dishes.

**Plátano (plantain):** A relative of the banana, which it resembles, although its flesh is thicker and its fruit is larger and not as sweet. Plantains can be prepared when green, ripe, or very ripe. Though they are classified as a fruit, when green, plantains are eaten as a vegetable in Cuba.

**Pressure Cooker Method for Cooking Dried Beans:** Place the soaked beans and their soaking liquid in a pressure cooker. Add the bell pepper, garlic, and bay leaf to the pot. Lock the lid into place and set the petcock on the vent pipe. Place the cooker over medium-high heat; bring to full pressure and cook for 20 minutes (or follow the manufacturer's directions for your own pressure cooker). Remove the cooker from the heat and allow the steam to dissipate. After about 15 minutes, with your hand protected by an oven mitt, carefully lift off the petcock. If no steam comes out of the vent, carefully remove the lid. If there is still steam emerging, wait until it stops before opening the cooker.

**Quimbombo (okra):** A vegetable of African origin with green rocket-shaped pods. In Cuba, okra is used in rice dishes and in soups and stews. When buying fresh okra, choose the smallest unblemished pods. Frozen okra may be substituted, but do not thaw before cooking.

**Ron (rum):** A distilled liquor made from the molasses that is a by-product of sugar production. Cuba is famous for its light-bodied young white rum that mixes well with fruit juices, but also produces darker fuller bodied *añejo* and other aged rums.

**Sofrito:** Sauté of onions, tomatoes, pepper, garlic, herbs, and spices, used as the basis of many Cuban creole dishes.

**Tasajo (salt-dried beef):** *Tasajo* must be soaked overnight in several changes of water to remove the salt before it is cooked. This method of preserving meat dates back to a time before refrigeration. *Tasajo* has a distinctive flavor and is still sold in Cuban grocery stores. If it is not available, however, substitute fresh beef brisket.

**Tocino (slab bacon):** Smoked bacon sold unsliced and used for seasoning.

**Tostones:** Twice-fried green plantains.

**Viandas:** Starchy tubers, such as *malanga, boniato,* yuca, *ñame,* and potatoes, used in Cuban cooking.

**Yuca, cassava, or manioc:** A root vegetable that has been a Cuban staple since pre-Columbian times. There are two basic varieties, bitter and sweet. The bitter variety contains a high level of prussic acid and is toxic if not properly prepared. First it must be completely peeled, then the white flesh grated and all of the juices pressed out. Cuba's original Native American inhabitants dipped the points of their arrows in this poisonous liquid. The detoxified flesh is then pounded and made into an unleavened crackerlike bread called *casabe.* Sweet yuca, the kind sold fresh in supermarket produce departments, should also be carefully peeled to remove both the outer brown peel and pink underpeel. The white flesh is boiled before eating. Sweet yuca has a texture and flavor similar to those of a potato. It can be boiled, added to soups, made into fritters or croquettes, or fried as chips or in chunks. In Cuba, boiled yuca is often served with *mojo* sauce.

# Bibliography

Abella Forcada, Ramona V. *From Cuba with Love*. New York: iUniverse, 2003.

Bolívar Aróstegui, Natalia, and Carmen Gonzáles Díaz De Villegas. *Afro-Cuban Cuisine*. Havana: Editorial José Martí, 1998.

*Cocina al minuto*. Miami, FL: Ediciones CUBAMERICA.

Creen, Linette. *A Taste of Cuba*. New York: Penguin, 1991.

*The Cuban Flavor*. Miami, FL: Downtown Book Center, 1979.

De La Grana Quintana, Aurora. *La cocina y usted*. Havana: ADIEDO.

Faya, Alberto. *El libro del sabor*. Havana: Ediciones UNION, 1999.

González, Reynaldo. *¡Eschale salsita!* Havana: Lo Real Maravilloso, 2000.

González-Hastings, Josefa. *The Habana Café Cookbook*. Gainsville: University Press of Florida, 2004.

Lafray, Joyce. *¡Cuba Cocina!* New York: William Morrow, 2001.

Lindgren, Glen, Raul Musibay, and Jorge Castillo. *Three Guys from Miami Cook Cuban*. Salt Lake City, UT: Gibbs Smith, 2004.

Llamas, Beatriz. *Taste of Cuba*. New York: Interlink, 2005.

Lluriá de O'Higgins, María Josefa. *A Taste of Old Cuba*. New York: HarperCollins, 1994.

Manual Reyes Corona, Pedro. *Nuestra cocina*. 2nd ed. Havana: Editorial Cientfico-Técnica, 1999.

Menéndez, Ana. *In Cuba I Was a German Shepherd*. New York: Grove, 2001.

*Old Havana Cookbook*. 3rd ed. New York: Hippocrene, 2000.

Parkinson, Rosemary. *Culinaria: The Caribbean*. Köln: Könemann, 1999.

Perez, Yoly N. *Café Mima Cuban Cookbook*. [Yolanda Perez]**,** 1998.

Raichlen, Steven. *The Caribbean Pantry Cookbook*. New York: Artisan, 1995.

Rodriguez, Douglas. *Nuevo Latino*. Berkeley, CA: Ten Speed Press, 2002.

Sarmiento Ramírez, Ismael. *Cuba*. Aldabada Ediciones.

Urrutia Randelman, Mary, and Joan Schwartz. *Memories of a Cuban Kitchen*. New York: Wiley, 1992.

Vásquez Gálvez, Madelaine. *Cocina ecólogica en Cuba*. Havana: Editorial José Martí, 2002.

Villapol, Nitza. *Cocina criolla*. Mexico, D.F.: Berbera Editores S.A. de C.V.

# Sources for Cuban Cooking Ingredients

*Many ingredients used in Cuban recipes may be found in your local super- or Latino food market. The following sources offer retail, wholesale, online, or mail-order sales; contact each company for more information.*

**Amigofoods.com**
7501 NE 3rd Place
Miami, FL 33138
Phone: (800) 627-2544
Fax: (516) 627-0803
Web: http://store.amigofoods.com
E-mail: customerservice@amigofoods.com

Online grocery store carrying Cuban-style foods and seasonings including black beans, picadillo, chorizo, *bacalao*, sofrito, *mojo*, yuca, and more, from popular brands such as El Ebro, Malta Hatuey, Pilon, Materva, El Criollo, and Chef Cesar.

**Brooks Tropicals**
P.O. Box 900160
Homestead, FL 33090
Phone: (305) 247-3544 or (800) 327-4833
Fax: (305) 246-5827
Web: www.brookstropicals.com
E-mail: info@brookstropicals.com

Harvests and/or imports more than thirty tropical fruits and vegetables, including *boniato*, calabaza, carambola (star fruit), chayote, coconut, ginger, kumquat, lime, lychee, *malanga*, mamey sapote, mango, *ñame*, papaya, plantain, sugarcane, water coconut, and yuca.

**The Caribbean Market**
7505 New Hampshire Avenue
Takoma Park, MD 20912
Phone: (301) 439-5288
Fax: (301) 439-5283
Web: www.thecaribbeanmarket.com
E-mail: inquiries@thecaribbeanmarket.com

West Indian grocery with freshly made Caribbean dishes and baked goods for take-out. Grocery items include fresh fruits and vegetables such as breadfruit, callaloo, *dasheen* (*eddo*), plantains, and yams; herbs, spices, and sauces; and fresh meat and fish.

**Compare Supermarket**
1870 Providence Boulevard
Deltona, FL 32725
Phone: (386) 789-3289

Hispanic market carrying plantains, banana leaves, rice dishes, Cuban bread, and more. Several Florida locations.

**La Criolla Grocery**
4940 Lake Underhill Road
Orlando, FL 32807
Phone: (407) 275-5580

Grocery carrying Cuban and Caribbean products, including beans, rice, sandwiches, meats, and beverages.

**Cuban Food Market**
(See Sentir Cubano)
Web: www.cubanfoodmarket.com

**Dean and Deluca**
560 Broadway
New York, NY 10012
Phone: (212) 226-6800
Web: www.deandeluca.com

A general gourmet food market, Dean and Deluca does carry fresh seafood and Spanish herbs and spices. Multiple locations nationwide; check website for store locations.

**La Española Meats, Inc.**
25020 Doble Avenue
Harbor City, CA 90710
Phone: (310) 539-0455
Fax: (310) 539-5989
Web: www.laespanolameats.com
E-mail: info@laespanolameats.com

Importer, wholesaler, and distributor with a retail deli and online ordering. Spanish-style chorizos, sausages, hams, salt cod, cheeses, olive oil, rice, and sweets.

**Frieda's Inc.**
Web: www.friedas.com

Exotic and specialty produce including *boniatos*, bananas and plantains, citrus, guava, mangoes, chiles, yuca, calabaza, and more. Their branded products are available through local supermarket and specialty markets; check website for store locations.

**Goya Foods**
Web: www.goya.com

Caribbean items include *bacalao*, guava paste, sofrito, bean and rice mixes, coconut milk, and papaya and guava products. The brand is carried in local grocery stores and supermarket chains throughout the United States, Puerto Rico, and in international markets. Check website for contact information for regional distributors. Online shopping through the website is planned.

**Kalustyan's**
123 Lexington Avenue
New York, NY 10016
Phone: (212) 685-3451
Web: www.kalustyans.com

Yuca flour.

**Kingston-Miami Trading Co.**
280 NE 2nd Street
Miami, FL 33132
Phone: (305) 372-9547 or (800) 915-5678
Fax: (305) 381-6527
Web: www.kingstonmiami.com

Sauces, seasonings, beverages, syrups, coconut milk, jams and jellies, and canned fruits and vegetables.

**La Marqueta/Moore Street Market**
108 Moore Street
Brooklyn, NY 11206
Phone: (718) 384-1371

Merchants sell a wide range of ingredients for traditional Latin cooking, including fresh tropical fruit and vegetables; meat, poultry, and seafood; and deli items and prepared foods.

**Melissa's/World Variety Produce, Inc.**
P.O. Box 21127
Los Angeles, CA 90021
Phone: (800) 588-0151
Web: www.melissas.com
E-mail: hotline@melissas.com

Melissa's organic and exotic fruits, vegetables, and spices are available online through the website or in more than 150 supermarket chains, gourmet food shops, and specialty stores throughout the United States. Latin offerings include mangoes, mamey sapote, banana leaves, plantains, chiles, limes, and a "Cuban Roots Sampler" with about two pounds each of malanga, ñame, and boniato.

**Penzeys Spices**
Brookfield, WI
Phone: (800) 741-7787
Fax: (262) 785-7678
Web: www.penzeys.com

Online source for spices, seasonings, and herbs, including adobo, arrow-root, epazote, ginger, and Jamaican and Caribbean seasoning mixes.

**The Raymond-Hadley Corp.**
89 Tompkins Street
Spencer, NY 14883
Phone: (607) 589-4415 or (800) 252-5220
Fax: (607) 589-6442
Web: www.raymondhadley.com
E-mail: contact@raymondhadley.com

More than two hundred products from West Africa, Central America, Peru, and the Caribbean, including spices and seeds, cornmeal, plantain and other exotic flours, beans, and canned and bulk products.

**Red Apple Farmers Market**
7645 New Hampshire Avenue
Hyattsville, MD 20783
Phone: (301) 434-1810

West Indian market with callaloo, breadfruit, yams, calabaza, and herbs, along with fresh, pickled, and dried meats and codfish.

**Sentir Cubano**
3100 SW 8th Street
Miami, FL 33135
Phone: (305) 644-8870 or (877) 999-9945
Web: www.sentircubano.com

Owners Miguel and Maria Vazquez operate a retail store, Sentir Cubano, and an online shopping site, www.cubanfoodmarket.com, with more than two thousand fresh and packaged Cuban grocery products, including fish and meats, *boniatos*, chorizos and *tasajo*, guava paste and shells, Cuban coffees and beverages, crackers, rice mixes, condiments such as *bijol*, and frozen foods including frozen fresh tropical fruit pulps (mamey sapote, *guanábana*, and so on) for use in drinks, ice creams, and sorbets.

**Toronto Caribbean Corner**
171 Baldwin Street
Toronto, ON M5T 1L9 Canada
Phone: (416) 593-0008

This deli carries salt cod, yams, plantains, Scotch bonnet peppers, whole fresh *guanábana*, *dasheen*, and callaloo.

**La Unica Food Mart**
1515 W. Devon Avenue
Chicago, IL 60660
Phone: (773) 274-7788

Cuban grocery store that also prepares food for dine-in or take-out. Menu items include fried yellow plantains, *yuca con mojo*, and Cuban coffee.

**Your DeKalb Farmer's Market**
3000 E. Ponce De Leon Avenue
Decatur, GA 30030
Phone: (404) 377-6400
Web: www.dekalbfarmersmarket.com

Huge farmers market and gourmet grocery store with an international flavor. Produce, meats and seafood, spices, baked goods, and beverages are among the offerings.

# Some Favorite Places for Eating Cuban

## In and around Havana

*Please note: telephone numbers in Cuba are not consistent in their number of digits.*

**Bedegon Onda**
Rustic tavern belonging to the Hotel Comendador in Old Havana. Menu includes Spanish tapas like potato and chorizo omelets. Also delicious grilled beef steaks served on a wooden trencher with roast potatoes and tomato and cucumber salad.

**Obrapía**
No. 55, La Havana Vieja
Phone: 867-1037

**El Buganvil Restaurante**
190, No. 1501, between 15th and 17th, Siboney, Central Habana
Phone: 271-4791

A good, low-key restaurant with a pretty garden.

**Paladar la Guarida**
Concordia No. 418, between Gervasio and Escobar, Havana
Phone: 866-9047

Best example of new-wave Cuban cooking in Havana. Owners Enrique Nuñez and Odesis Baullosa, working with Chef Manuel Antonio Sid Ibañez, turn out some of the most well executed and original dishes in Havana. The award-winning movie *Fresas y chocolate* (*Strawberries and Chocolate*) was filmed here.

**Paladar la Esperanza**
Calle 16, No. 105, between Ira and 3rd, Miramar
Phone: 202-4361

This charming restaurant is located in a stylish, eclectically decorated house. The menu includes whatever is good at the market that day. Hubert, at the front of the house, and Chef Manolo, in the kitchen, do a good job.

**Hurón Azul Restaurant Paladar**
Humbolt, No. 153, corner of P. El Vedado, Havana
Phone: 879-1691
E-mail: dehuronazul@hotmail.com

This tiny restaurant is a gathering place for Cuban artists. Paintings by some of Cuba's most famous painters line the walls. The food is a combination of beautifully prepared classics like *masitas de puerco* and black beans and rice and interesting innovations.

**La Finca (La Casa de Erasmo)**
Calle 190 and 19, Rpto. Cubanacan, Havana
Phone: 208-7976

Internationally known chef Erasmo presides over the kitchen of this attractive restaurant located in a small house with terraces and exotic tropical gardens where pigeons coo. The menu is both classic and eclectic, while being rooted in creole cooking. It is expensive, but not outrageous.

### El Aljibe
Avenue 7ma., between 24th and 26th, Miramar, Havana
Phone: 241584 or 241583

This popular, moderately priced restaurant has been in the same family for three generations. It is famous for its garlic roast chicken.

### Paladar La Cocina de Lilliam
Calle 48, No. 1311, between 13th and 15th, Miramar, Havana
Phone: 209-6514

Good classic creole cooking in a pleasant garden setting.

### Eco-Restaurante El Bambú
Jardin Botanico Nacional, Can Expocuba, Havana
Phone: 547-278

An innovative new-wave vegetarian restaurant located in the Japanese Gardens of the National Botanical Gardens. Open for lunch.

### Paladar Vistamar
Avenida 1ra., No. 2206, between 22nd and 24th, Miramar, Havana
Phone: 23-8328

A small, stylish restaurant in a spectacular 1950s modern house with a spectacular view of Havana Bay. Good food and great service.

## On the road between Havana and Piñar del Rio:

### La Casa de Campesino
Autopista Nacional Havana, Piñar de Rio, Candelaria, Piñar del Rio
Phone: (82) 77-8700

A traditional country-style restaurant located on a small farm in a national park that was once a French-owned coffee plantation. Good food in a pretty garden setting.

## Near Camaguey:

### Rambos S.A. Restaurant Oasis
Carreterra Central km. 18, Ciego de Avila
Phone: 2663361 or 28738

Located about one hour west of Camaguey, this is an outdoor restaurant on a working farm. The pork, chicken, and vegetables and fruits are either home grown or locally produced. The menu features good, simple food, well prepared.

## In the United States:

### Versailles Restaurant and Bakery
3555 S.W. 8th Street, Miami, Florida 33135
Phone (305) 444-0240 or (305) 445-7614

Miami's most famous classic Cuban restaurant. A good place for eating and people watching.

### Ola
425 Ocean Drive, Miami Beach, Florida 33139
Phone: (305) 695-9125

Cutting edge Nuevo Latino cooking with a Cuban beat. Internationally acclaimed Cuban-American chef restaurateur and cookbook author Douglas Rodriguez is a genie in the kitchen!

### The Habana Café
5402 Gulfport Blvd. South, Gulfport, Florida 33707
Phone: (727)-321-8855
www.habanacafe-usa.com

Chef and award winning cookbook author, Josefa "Jo" Gonzales-Hastings comes from a family of good cooks and many of the dishes featured on the menu at her restaurant in Gulfport, a suburb of St Petersburg, have evolved from old family recipes.

### La Ideal Sandwich Shop
2924 Tampa Bay Blvd., Tampa, Florida 33607
Phone: (813) 870-0150

This small, bustling café, located in what was once an old neighborhood grocery store, is a favorite gathering place for Tampa's Cuban community. La Ideal serves great sandwiches and other casual, hearty food.

### Zafra Kitchen
301 Willow Avenue, Hoboken, New Jersey 07030
Phone: (210) 610-9801

### Cucharamama
233 Clinton Street, Hoboken, New Jersey 07030
Phone: (201) 420-1700

Food historian and chef Maricel Presilla's restaurants Zafra, and Cucharamama in Hoboken, New Jersey, have a strong local following and have become destinations that draw New York foodies through the Lincoln Tunnel from Manhattan. Zafra, which means "sugar harvest" in Cuban, has a Classic and Nuevo Cubano menu. Cucharamama is Nuevo Latino with Cuban touches. Both are worth the journey!

# Index